AF587711

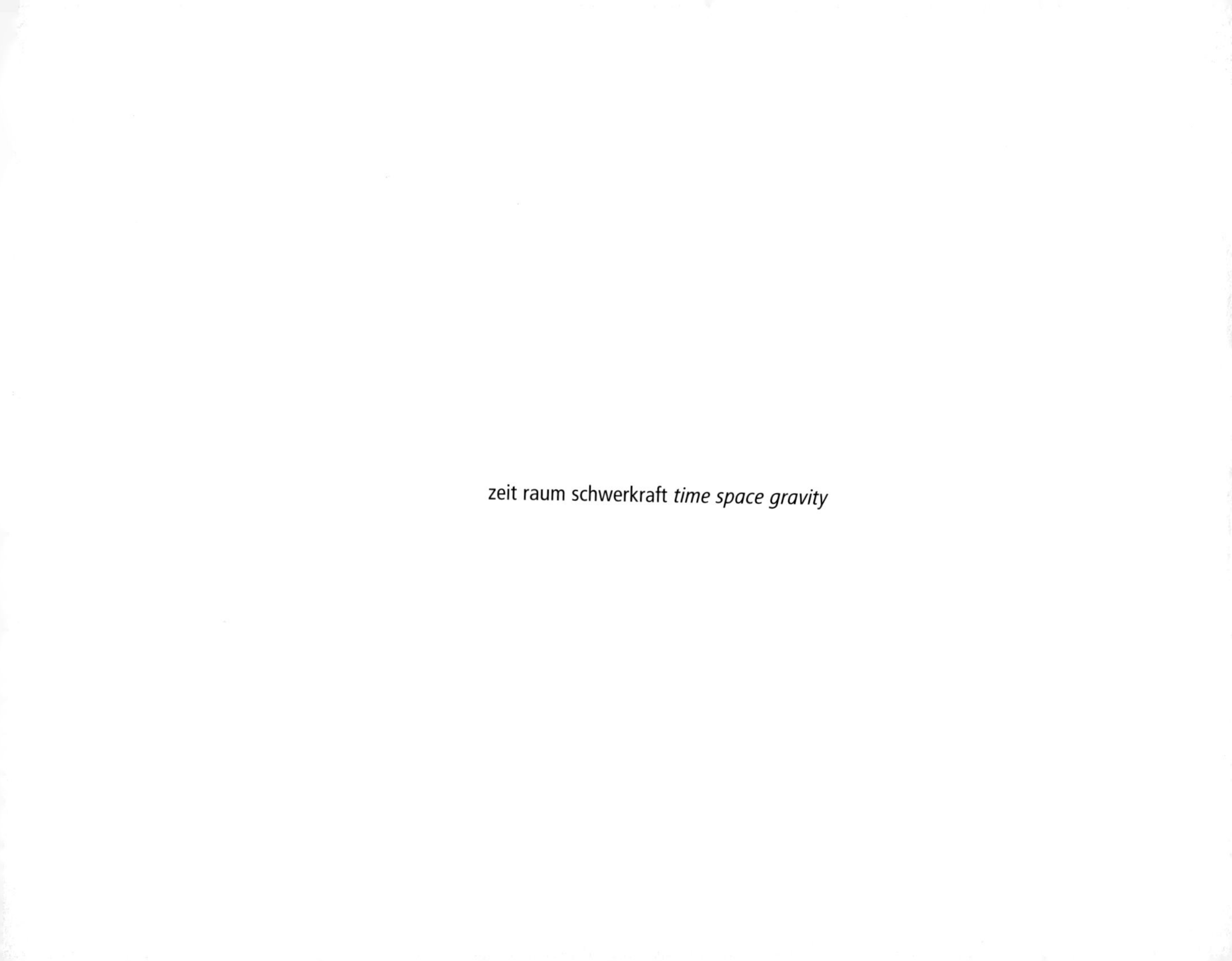

zeit raum schwerkraft *time space gravity*

edition axel menges

nicht identifiziert *unidentified*
© 2004 edition axel menges, stuttgart / london
isbn 3-932565-40-1

alle rechte vorbehalten, besonders die der übersetzung in andere sprachen.
all rights reserved, especially those of translation into other languages.

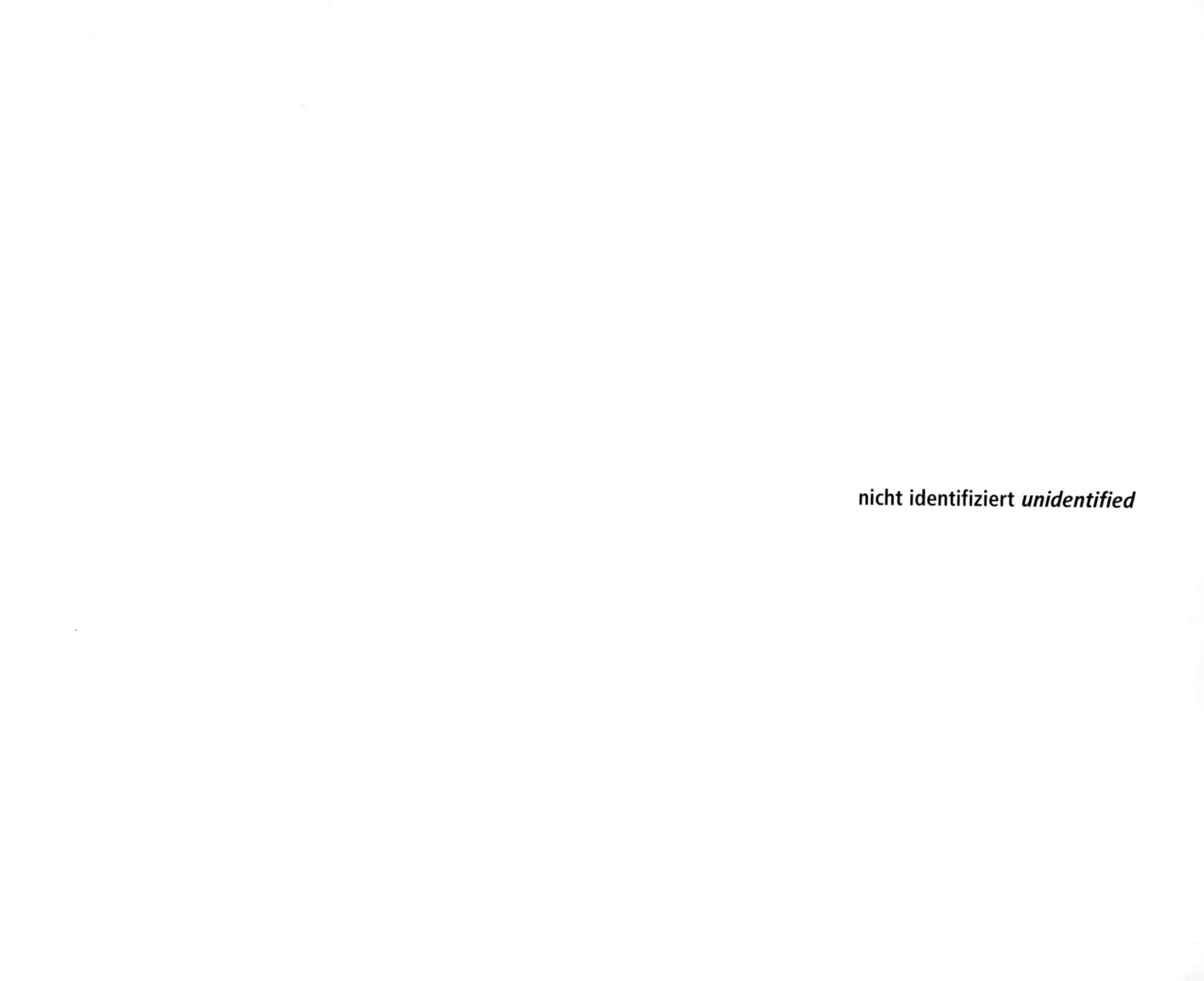

nicht identifiziert *unidentified*

gegeben ist nur die aufgabe. sie besteht aus dem thema «nicht identifiziert». keine weiteren einschränkungen, abgesehen von zeit, raum und schwerkraft.

«als ob dies nicht schon einschränkungen genug wären.» – «der raum selbst fordert heraus durch seine beschränkung.» – «nur 2,56 meter eng.» – «man könnte den raum eng nennen. man könnte auch sagen, es sei ein langer raum.»

Only the task is set. It consists of the topic, «unidentified». There are no further restrictions, apart from time, space and gravity.

«As if those weren't restrictions enough.» – «The room itself is a challenge in its restrictions.» – «Narrow – only 2.56 metres.» – «You could say, it's a narrow room, but you could also say, it's a long room.»

die aufgabe ist nicht die aufgabe. sie besteht eigentlich darin, selbst zu bestimmen, wohin der weg führen soll.

«das thema lautet ‹nicht identifiziert›.» – «warum?» – «in den jahren zuvor richtete sich das interesse meist auf die personen der designer, weniger auf die aussagen, die sie mit ihren entwürfen verbunden hatten. » – «also ist auch das teil der aufgabe: die auseinandersetzung mit den entwürfen, die bisher für diesen raum entwickelt worden waren.» – «das publikum vergleicht sofort.» – «was bleibt ihm anderes übrig?» – «eigene urteilskraft. oft ist es so, daß die besucher den entwurf so bewerten, als ob er keinen vorgänger hätte.» – «voraussetzungslos? zusammenhangslos? so wird kunst rezipiert. hier aber gibt es voraussetzungen und zusammenhänge, die berücksichtigt werden müssen. hier geht es um design.» – «zumindest geht es um antworten auf fragen, die einem designer gestellt werden.» – «wie lautete nochmal die frage, die mir gestellt wird?» – «nicht identfiziert.»

The problem is not the problem. The problem is to find the real problem, to set it yourself.

«The topic is ‹unidentified›.» – «Why?» – «In previous years, interest mainly focused on who the designers were and less on the messages they had incorporated in their designs.» – «So that's also part of the problem: getting to understand the designs that were previously produced for this room.» – «The audience compare them immediately.» – «What else could they do?» – «Use their own judgement. It's often the case that visitors assess the design as if nothing had gone before it.» – «Unconditionally? Totally out of context? That's how people judge art, but here there are preconditions and contexts which have to be taken into account. What we are dealing with here is design.» – «At least it's a matter of the answers to questions a designer is asked.» – «What was the question you were asking me again?» – «Unidentified.»

«warum gelb?» – «als mir die idee kam, war sie gelb. gedankenspiele mit orange oder grün sind gescheitert. farben, die ich sonst bevorzuge. es blieb gelb.» – «welche bedeutung hat die farbe für die installation?» – «gelb steht für energie, angefangen vom symbol für elektrischen strom bis zum warnzeichen für atomare strahlung. im comic werden gedankenblitze als gelb leuchtende glühbirnen gezeichnet.» – «energie, die innerhalb eines prozesses fließt, welcher in einer bahn gehalten und auf einen höhepunkt gelenkt wird?»

«Why yellow?» – «When it came to me in my mind it was yellow. I tried to change it to green and orange, colours I otherwise prefer, but it was yellow.» – «How important is the colour for the installation?» – «Yellow stands for energy, ranging from the symbol for electrical current to the warning sign for atomic radiation. In comics, brilliant ideas are drawn as bright yellow light bulbs.» – «Energy that flows within a process, that is kept in fixed channels and led to a climax?»

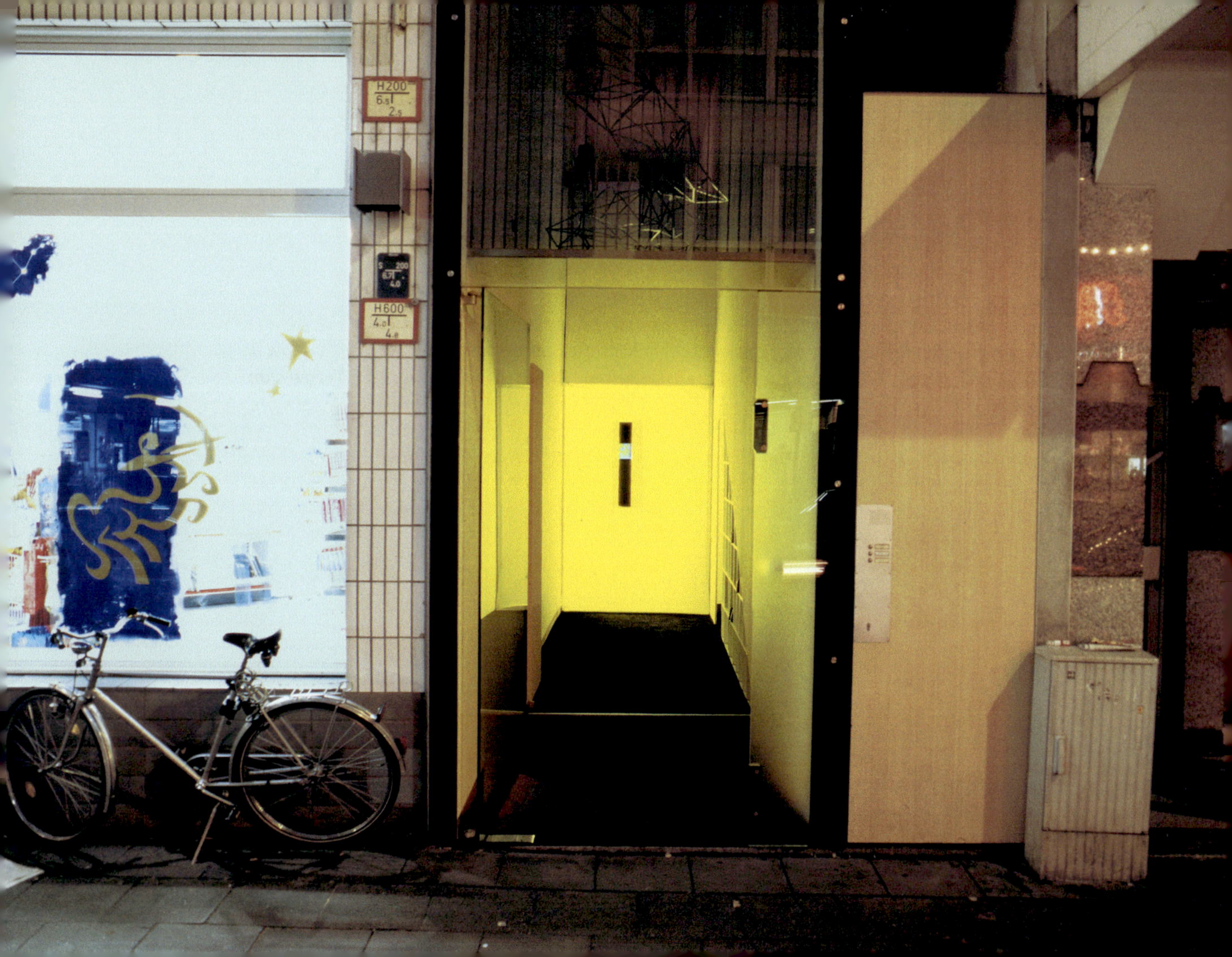
H200
6.5
2.5
H600
4.0
4.8

nach auskunft des deutschen wetterdienstes beträgt die aufgrund statistischer erfahrung zu erwartende temperatur in köln in der zweiten januarhälfte 7 grad celsius. die wahrscheinlichkeit, trockenen fußes zur ausstellung zu gelangen, liegt bei 23 prozent.

«es ist unangenehm, seine schuhe bei diesem mistwetter auch noch ausziehen zu müssen.» – «sich auf eine neue situation einzulassen, beginnt mit einer unangenehmen erfahrung. saturiertheit verhindert entdeckungen.»

According to the Meteorological Office, statistics show that the temperature to be expected in the second half of January in Cologne is 7 degrees Celsius. The probability of reaching the exhibition without getting your feet wet is 23 percent.

«It's unpleasant to have to take your shoes off in this lousy weather.» – «Confronting a new situation starts with an unpleasant experience. Saturation impedes discovery.»

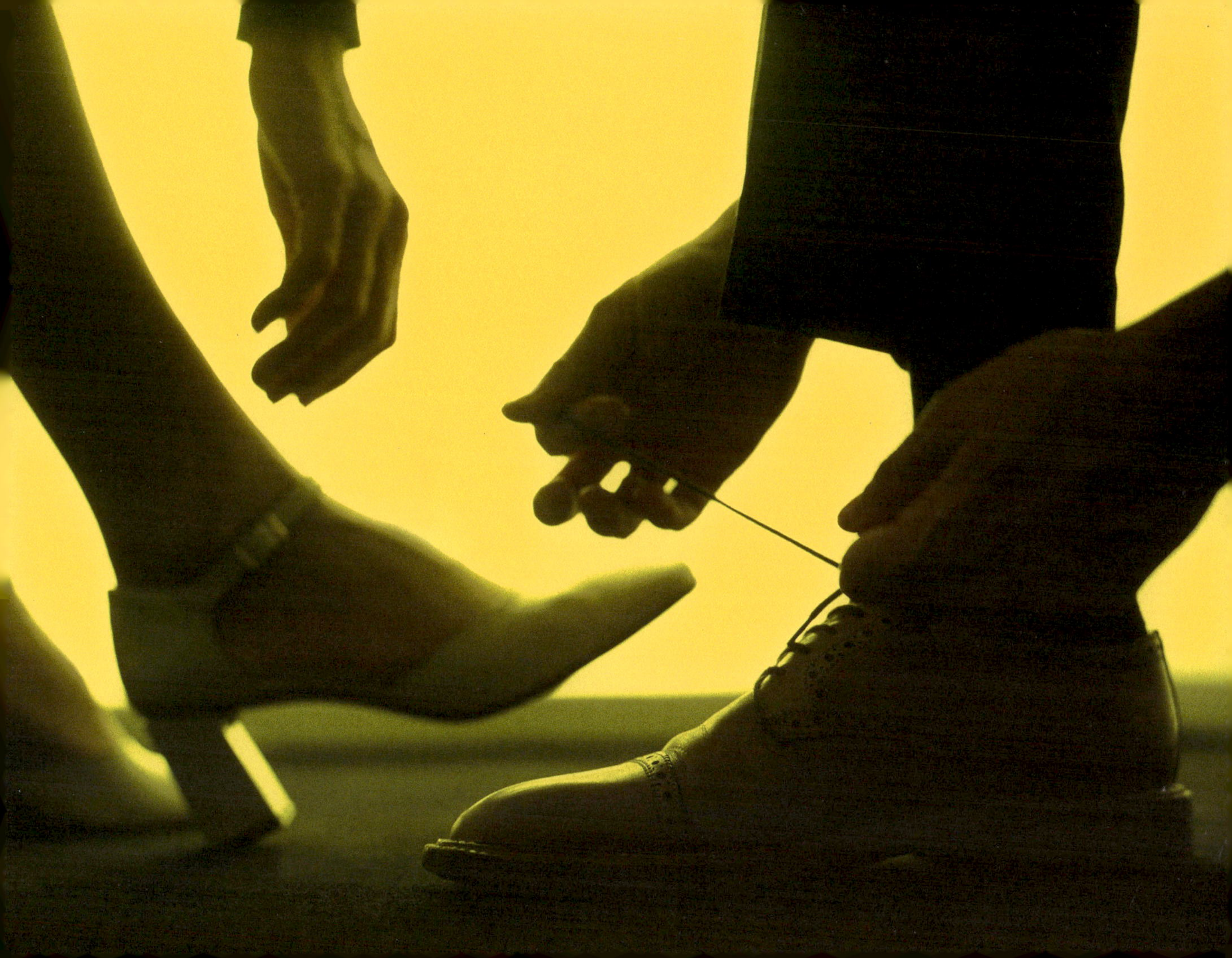

den besucher erwartet beim betreten des gebäudes eine leuchtend gelbe wand. eine öffnung gewährt eintritt – zu eng und unbequem scheint der durchgang, doch anziehend. bei den ersten, vorsichtigen schritten durch die gerade schulterbreite passage entdeckt er, daß die gelbe wand nachgibt und sich den bewegungen anpaßt. eigentlich ganz angenehm, ein wenig instabil, aber nicht gefährlich. die schritte hinterlassen spuren, die langsam verblassen und allmählich von den spuren der folgenden besucher überlagert werden. nach wenigen minuten ist die oberfläche wieder im ursprünglichen zustand, die spuren sind verschwunden.

When entering the building, the visitor finds himself confronted with a bright yellow wall: only a narrow entrance allows them to enter the passage – almost too small to squeeze through, yet strongly appealing. Taking the first careful steps through this narrow passage, one discovers that the yellow wall gives and adjusts to movements. In fact it is quite comfortable, a bit unstable, but not dangerous. The footsteps leave behind traces that slowly dim, to be overlaid and covered by the footsteps of those following. Only a few minutes later, the surface regains its original position, and the traces have disappeared.

«wie sehr muß ich einsinken, mich in den entwurf vertiefen?» – «es geht weniger um die tiefe als um die unsicherheit und sanftheit. boden und wände sind eher wabbelig als hart.» – «rahmenbedingungen im design sind nicht hart?»

«How deep do I have to sink to delve into the design?» – «It's no so much a matter of depth: more of insecurity and cosiness. The floor and walls are wobbly rather than hard.» – «So the general set-up of the design isn't hard?»

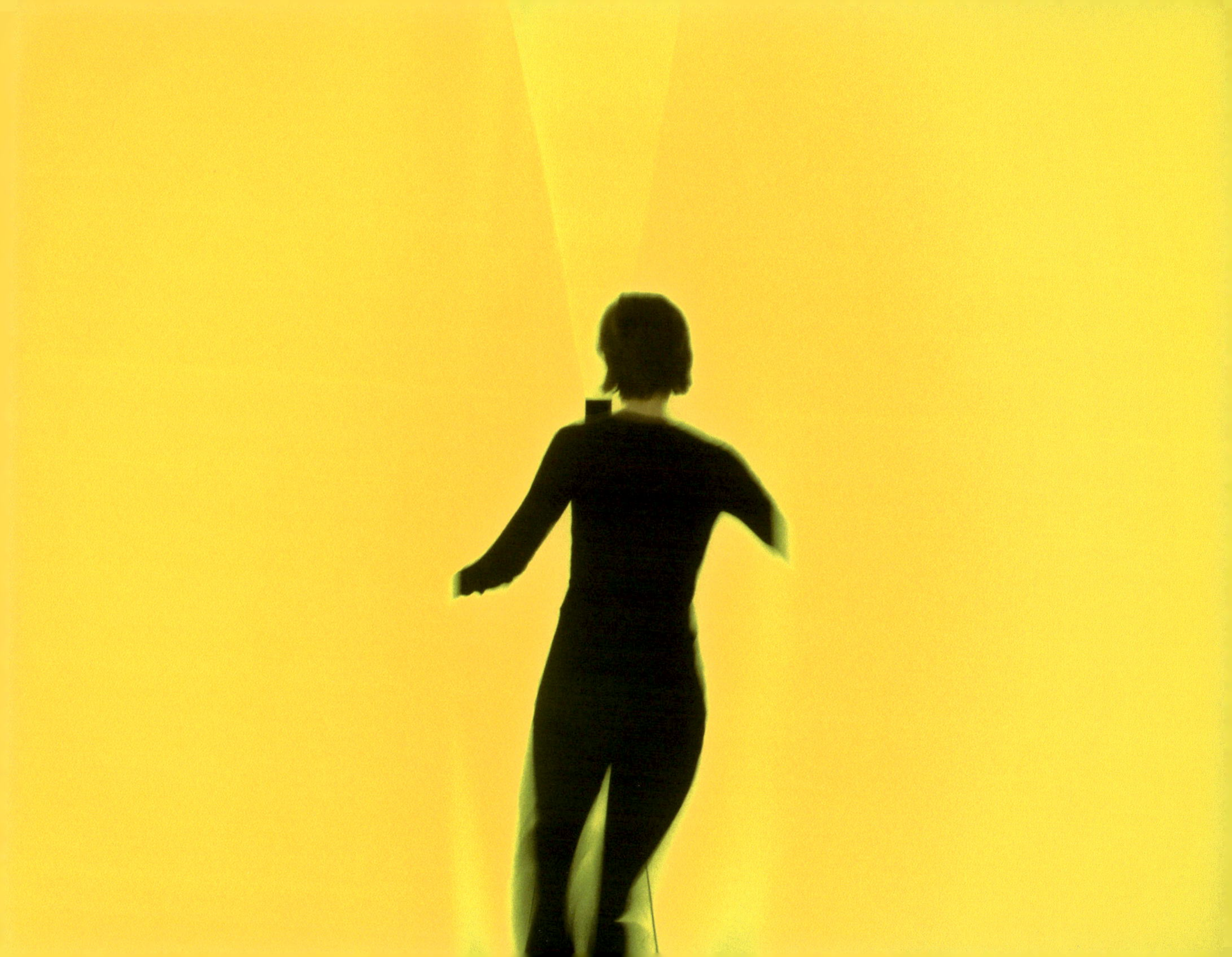

genau genommen eine zumutung, daß der besucher die bequemlichkeit mit seinen schuhen ablegen und sich durch einen begrenzten gang hindurchzwängen muß.

«um zu erkunden, welche möglichkeit wirklich in einem medium steckt, muß man seine bequemlichkeit, seine gewohnheiten aufgeben.» – «die gelbe passage als medium?» – «medium und rahmen zugleich. wir brauchen eine strategie als rahmen, damit wir tatsächlich verstehen, was wir tun.» – «im unterschied zum künstler, der spontan das macht, wozu er lust hat?» – «die gelbe passage ist die palette der möglichkeiten, die jedem besucher zur verfügung steht: hier tritt jeder auf.» – «um aufzutreten, muß man unsicheren boden betreten?»

To put a fine point on it, it's an imposition for the visitors to cast off their laziness with their shoes and squeeze themselves through a delimited passage.

«To discover what opportunities a medium really offers, you have to step out of your comfort zone.» – «The yellow passage as a medium?» – «A medium and a framework at the same time. We need a strategy as framework if we are really to understand what we are doing.» – «In contrast to the artist, who spontaneously does whatever he pleases?» – «The yellow passage is the palette of possibilities open to every visitor. Everyone performs here.» – «To perform, you have to set your foot on uncertain ground?»

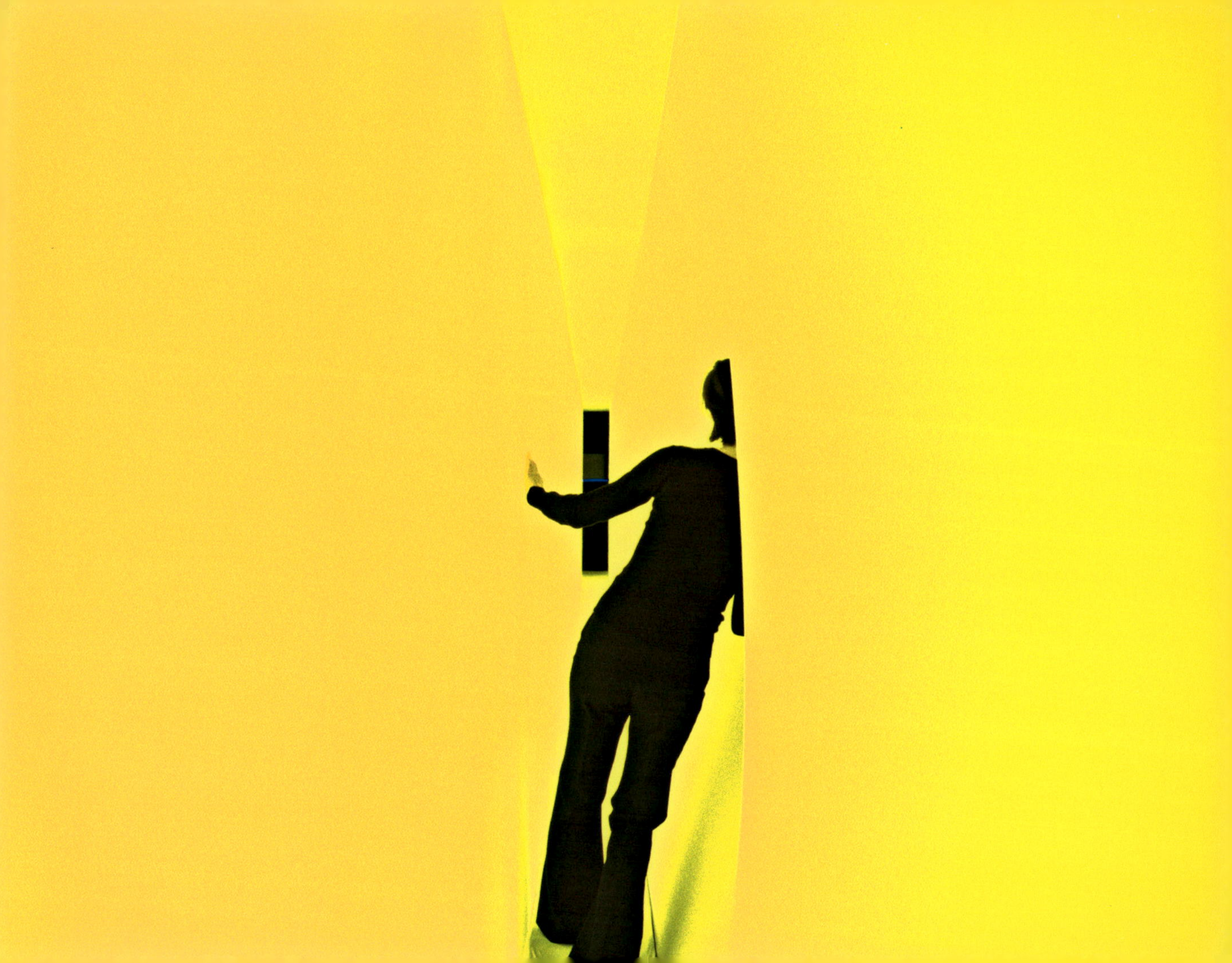

«wenn es ein medium gibt, dann gibt es auch einen inhalt.» – «selbst die ausstellung ist ein medium.» – «und ihr inhalt?» – «eine diskussion über design. über das leben. und darüber, was design mit unserem leben zu tun hat.» – «existentielle aspekte.» – «auch eine diskussion über die geschwindigkeit von design, über zeit, über inhalte, über den mangel an inhalten, über das desinteresse an inhalten. und darüber, was ein medium ist. der designbegriff muß neu definiert werden, weil er heute mißverstanden wird.» – «worin besteht hier deine mission?» – «täglich versuche ich menschen klarzumachen, daß wir uns, bevor wir etwas machen, über inhalt und medium klar werden müssen.»

«If there is a medium, then there is also content.» – «Even the exhibition is a medium.» – «And its content?» – «A discussion about design. About life and what design has to do with our lives.» – «Existential aspects.» – «Also a discussion about the speed of design, about time, about content, about the lack of content, about the lack of interest in content, and about what a medium is. The concept of design has to be redefined, because it is currently misunderstood.» – «What is your mission in this context?» – «Day by day, I try to make people understand that we have to understand the content and the medium before we do anything.»

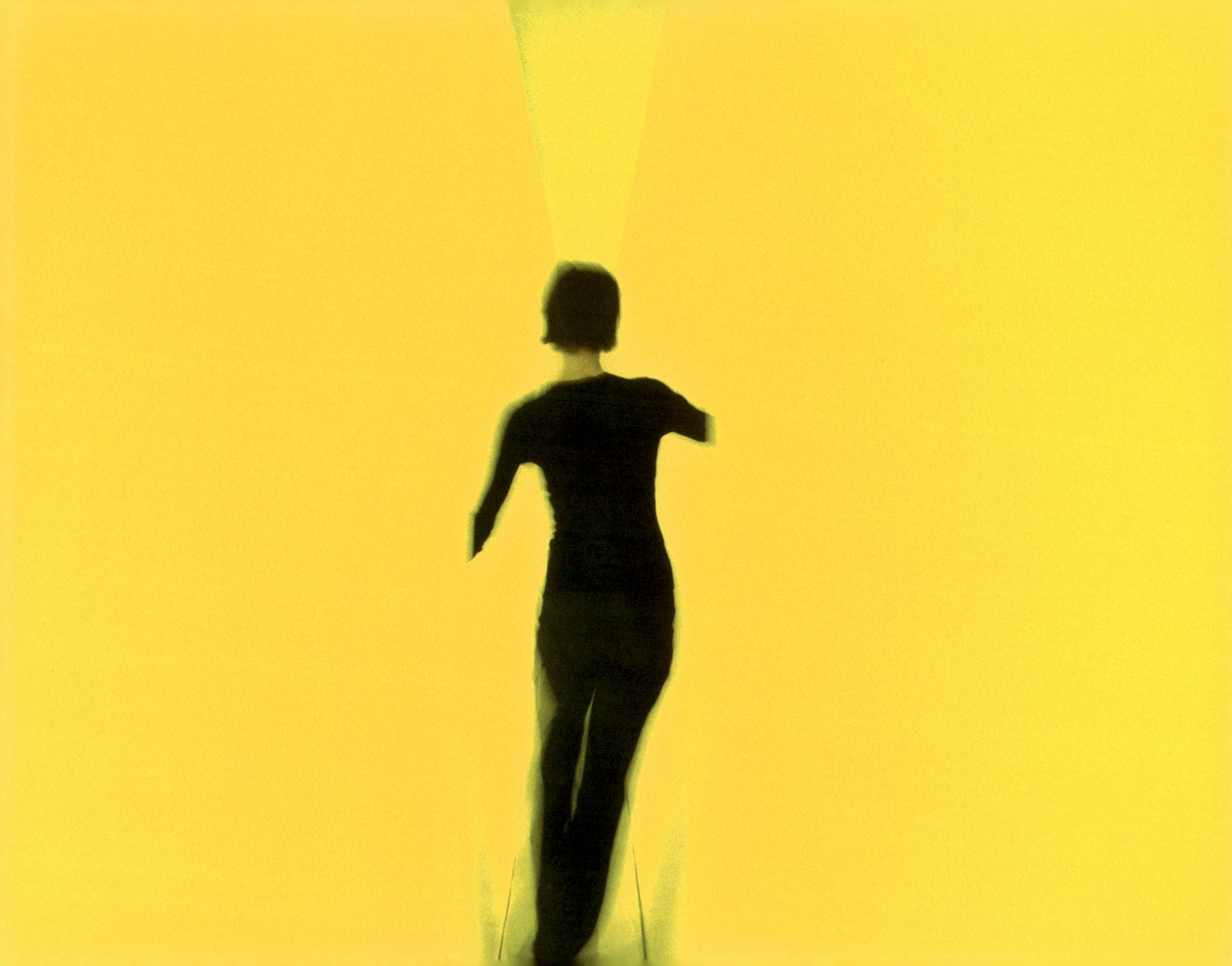

«hier geht es um ‹was› und ‹warum›, nicht um ‹wie› und ‹wer›.» – «geht es aber im design nicht stets darum, wer der designer ist?»

«So it's a matter of ‹what› and ‹why›, not ‹how› and ‹who›.» – «But in design, isn't the main thing always who the designer is?»

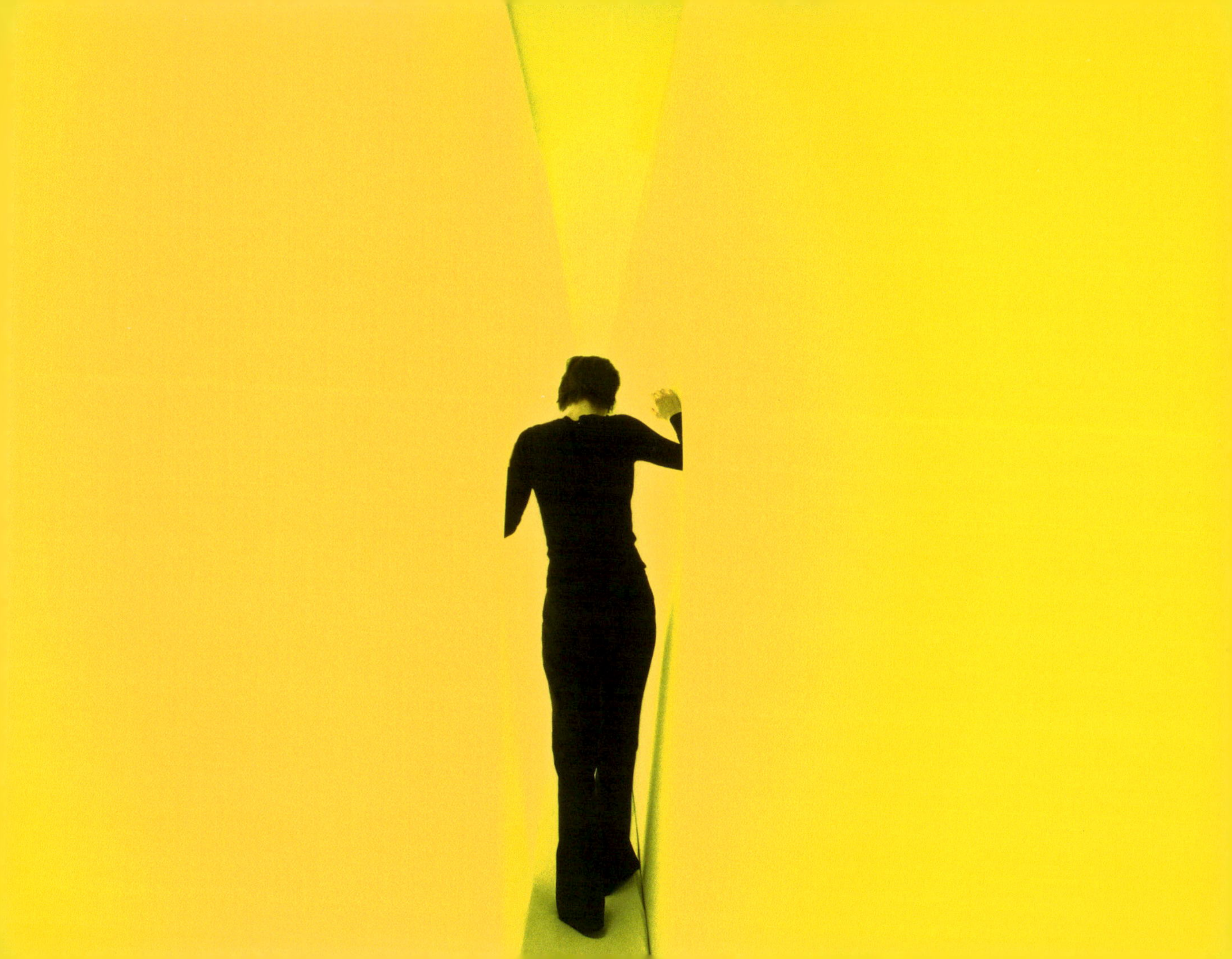

medium ist auch das material, der stoff, die elastische wand, die oberfläche.

«nicht, um zu belehren, sondern um energie zu wecken.» – «ein gelber stachel aus stoff?» – «die besucher sollen sich dazu angeregt fühlen, sich auf den weg zu machen. die möglichkeiten zu sehen, die um sie herum bestehen.» – «welche botschaft vermittelt das medium?» – «das material erzählt die geschichte: wer das medium versteht, kann es dem entsprechend einsetzen, wie das publikum es wahrnimmt.»

The medium is also the material, the fabric, the elastic wall, the surface.

«Not to educate, but to energise.» – «A yellow spur of fabric?» – «The visitors should feel inspired to be pioneers, to see the opportunities that surround them.» – «What message does the medium put across?» – « The material is telling the story: If you understand the medium you can use it in the way the public understands it.»

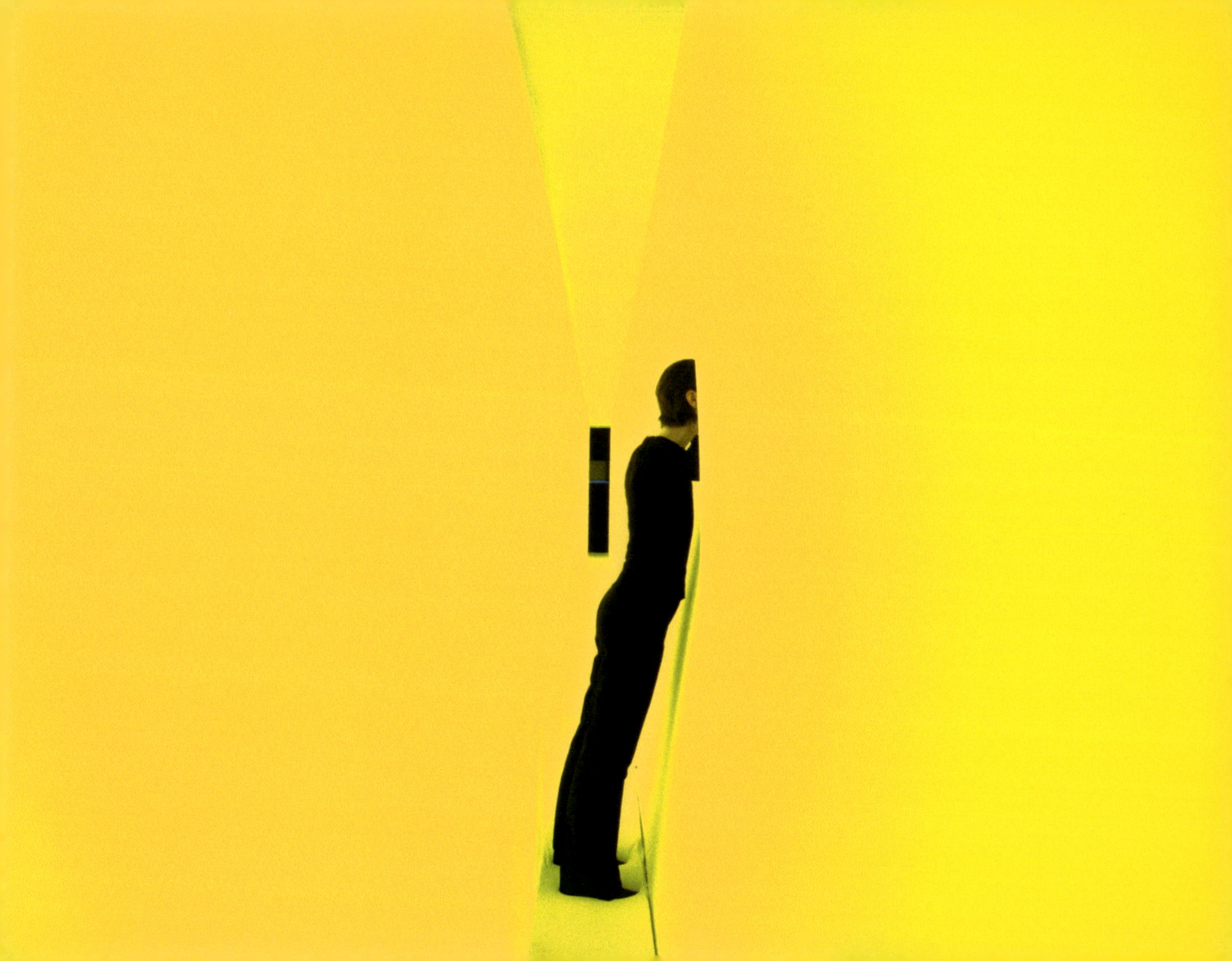

«nicht nur eine zeitung, eine zeitschrift, ein fernsehkanal, ein radioprogramm ist ein medium?» – «auch ein sessel ist ein medium. ein anderes als ein motorrad oder ein stift.» – «worin liegt der unterschied?» – «wir brauchen unterschiedliche talente oder werkzeuge, um mit den verschiedenen medien zu arbeiten.» – «wissen das alle?» – «wären wir in der besten aller welten, dann hätten wir alle es verstanden. designer sind dabei jedoch sehr schlampig. sie machen immer dasselbe, egal, um welches medium es sich gerade handelt.» – «die gelbe passage als kommentar zur nachlässigkeit der designer?» – «eher ein signal an alle, die mit kommunikation zu tun haben.»

«Not only a newspaper, a magazine, a television channel or a radio programme is a medium?» – «An armchair is also a medium – a different one from a motorcycle or a pen.» – «What is the difference?» – «We need different talents or tools to work with the various media.» – «Does everyone know that?» – «If we were in the best of all possible worlds, we would all have understood that. Designers, however, are very sloppy. They always do the same things no matter what medium they are working with.» – «The yellow passage as a comment on the sloppiness of designers?» – «Rather a signal to everyone who has to do with communication.»

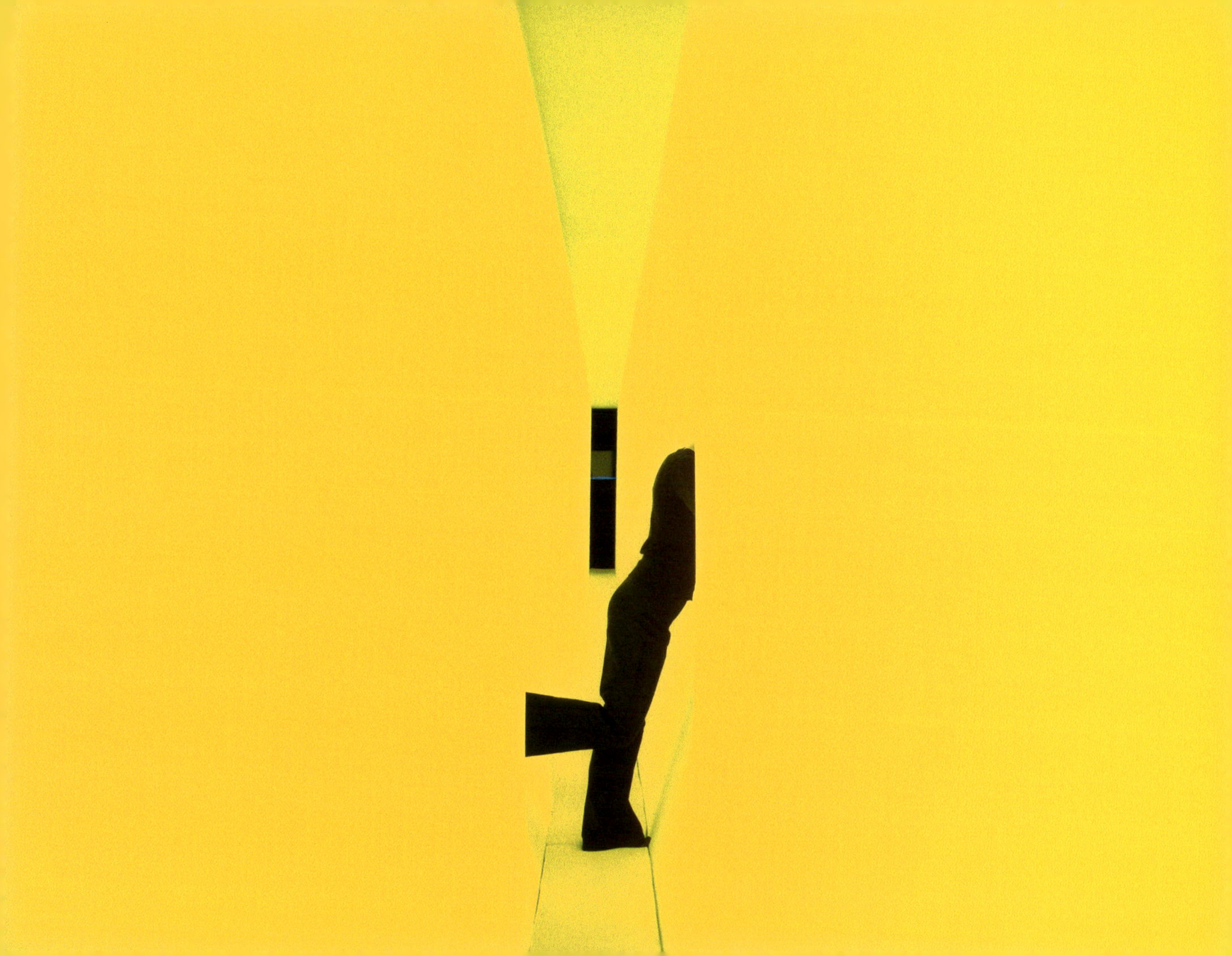

medium ist jedes element, das sich dazwischen befindet. das vermittelt. das eine botschaft übermittelt. in der physik und in der chemie eine substanz als träger bestimmter vorgänge: gas ist ein flüchtiges medium. in der medizin und parapsychologie ein wesen, das sich hypnotisieren läßt und verbindungen herstellt. im kaufhausregal ist es das buch oder die schallplatte, die der vermittlung von information, bildung und unterhaltung dient. im schaufenster ist es ein begriff für kommunikationsmittel, die zugleich auch werbeträger sein können: werbung als flüchtiger inhalt. zuletzt, stets im plural, ein kostspieliger organisatorischer und technischer apparat für die vermittlung von meinungen, informationen, kulturgütern gar.

«der zusammenhang zum design?» – «ein pädagogischer mehrwert. ich drücke damit aus, worum es im design eigentlich geht. objekte müssen als medien betrachtet werden. um was es sich bei der gestaltung unserer umwelt auch handelt (produkt, architektur, landschaft), es ist gestaltet, um eine botschaft zu vermitteln.»

Every element that is located in between is a medium. Everything that projects, or disseminates a message. In physics and chemistry, it is a substance which permits certain processes to take place: gas is a volatile medium. In medicine and parapsychology it is a being that allows itself to be hypnotised and establishes connections. On the shelves of department stores it is a book or a record, disseminating information, education or entertainment. In the shop window it is a term for means of communication which can also be advertising material: advertising as volatile contents. Finally, always in the plural, it is an expensive organisational and technical apparatus for the dissemination of opinions, information and even cultural assets.

«The connection with design?» – «Added pedagogical value. That sums up what design is really about. Objects have to be regarded as media. Whatever is designed in our environment (products, architecture or landscapes) is designed in order to put a message across.»

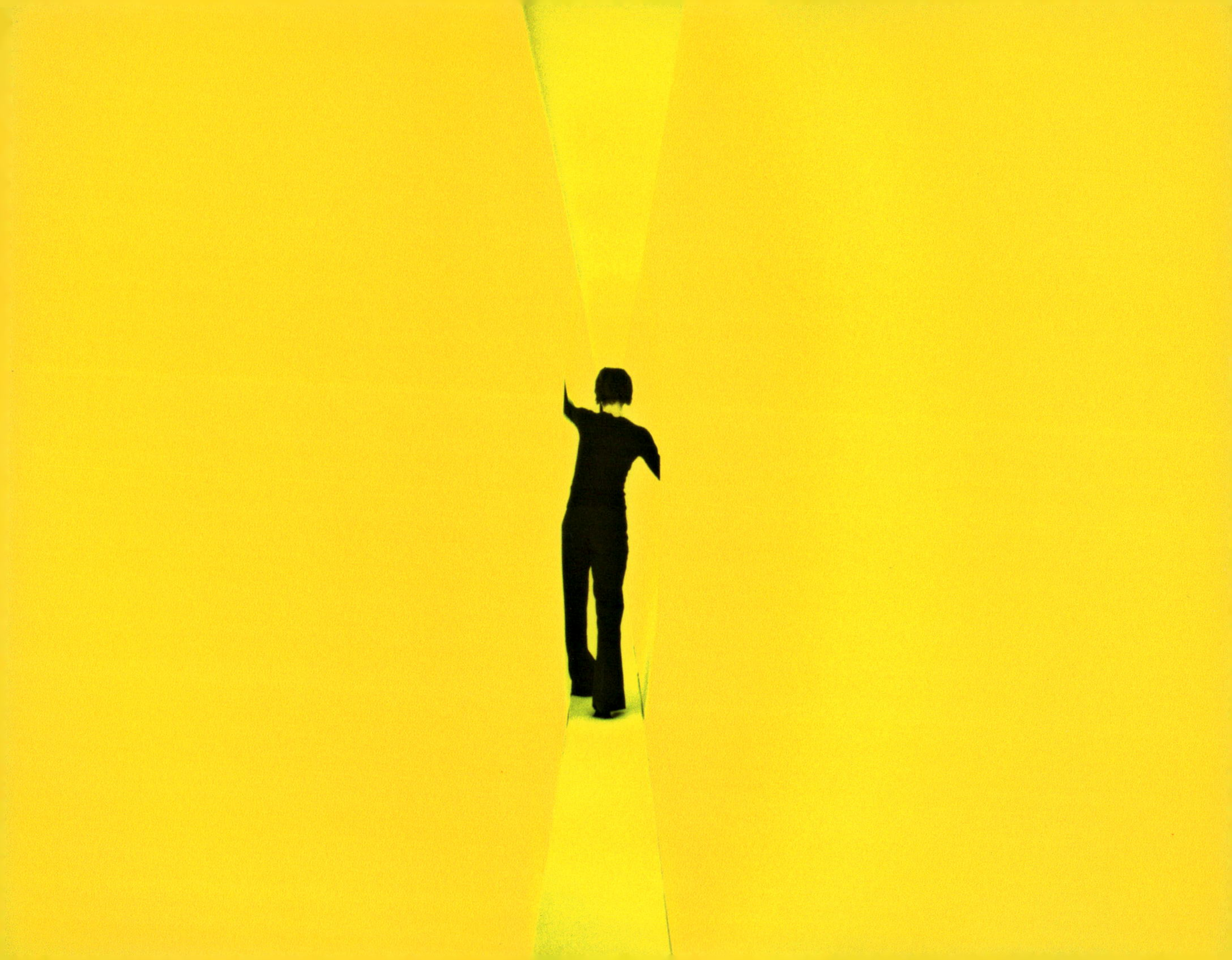

«und die eigentumsverhältnisse?» – «das hier ist sozusagen eine demokratische situation. die medien gehören jedermann.»

«And what about property rights?» – «This is really a very democratic situation. The media belong to everyone.»

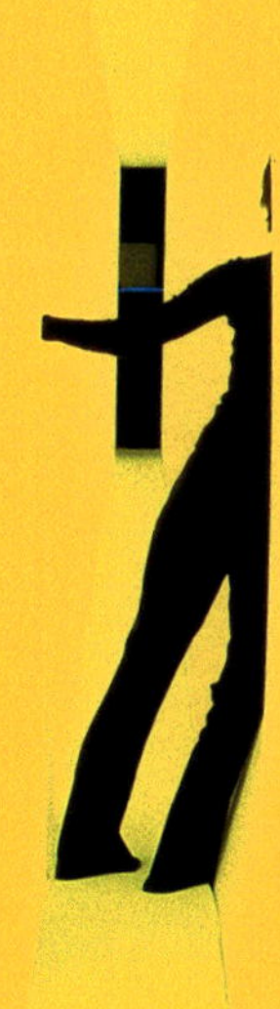

«also ist jeder ein designer?» – «jeder arbeitet als gestalter, mehr oder weniger absichtsvoll.» – «worin besteht dann die aufgabe des designers?» – «design bedeutet planung. es bedeutet, wohlüberlegt bestimmte physische aspekte eines unternehmens in einem zusammenhang erscheinen zu lassen, von welchem der designer überzeugt ist und von dem er glaubt, daß auch die kunden ihn wertschätzen. diese aufgabe ist unabhängig davon, ob das unternehmen schrauben oder autos herstellt. die gelbe wand ist in meinen augen ebenso ein medium wie eine schraube, ein stift oder eine flasche. wer sein medium planvoll und umsichtig einsetzt, wird erfolgreich sein.»

«So, is everyone a designer?» – «Everyone works as a designer, more or less intentionally.» – «What, then, does a real designer do?» – «Design means planning. It means deliberately forcing certain physical aspects of a company to appear in a context that the designer believes in, and that he believes the customers will appreciate. It doesn't matter whether the company produces screws or cars. To me, the yellow wall is the medium, just as would be a screw, or a pen, or a bottle. If you plan and use your media circumspectly, you will succeed.»

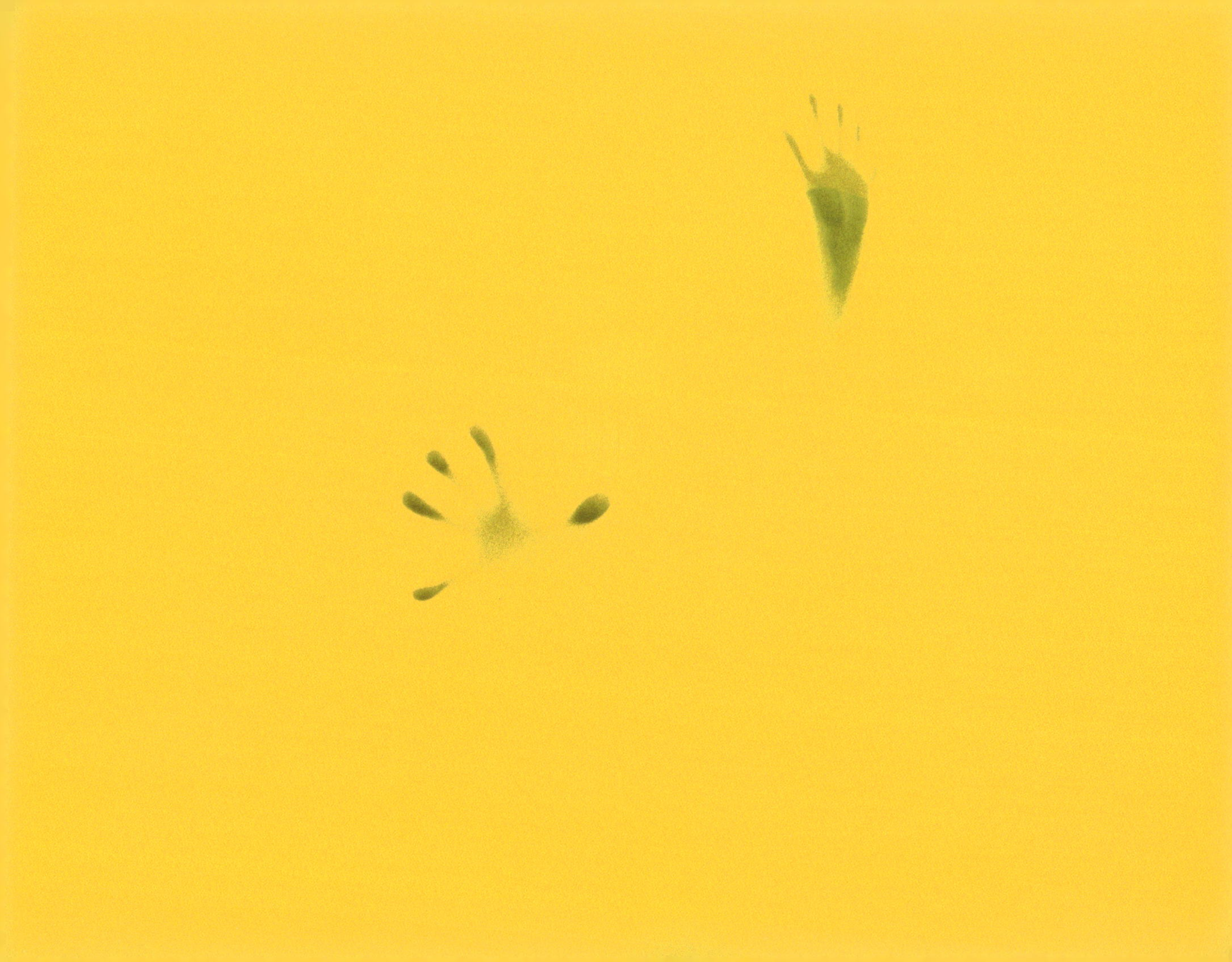

«wer nutzt sein spezifisches medium am besten?» – «das ist die herausforderung, die der markt an uns richtet. erfolgreich ist, wer sich mit herz und verstand seiner zielgruppe widmet. nur das design, das die medien seiner zeit am besten versteht, wird wirklich bahnbrechend neu sein.»

«Who is best at using the specific media?» – «That is the challenge the market faces us with. The successful one is the one who understands the mindset of his target group best. Making ground-breaking new design is understanding the media of that certain time best.»

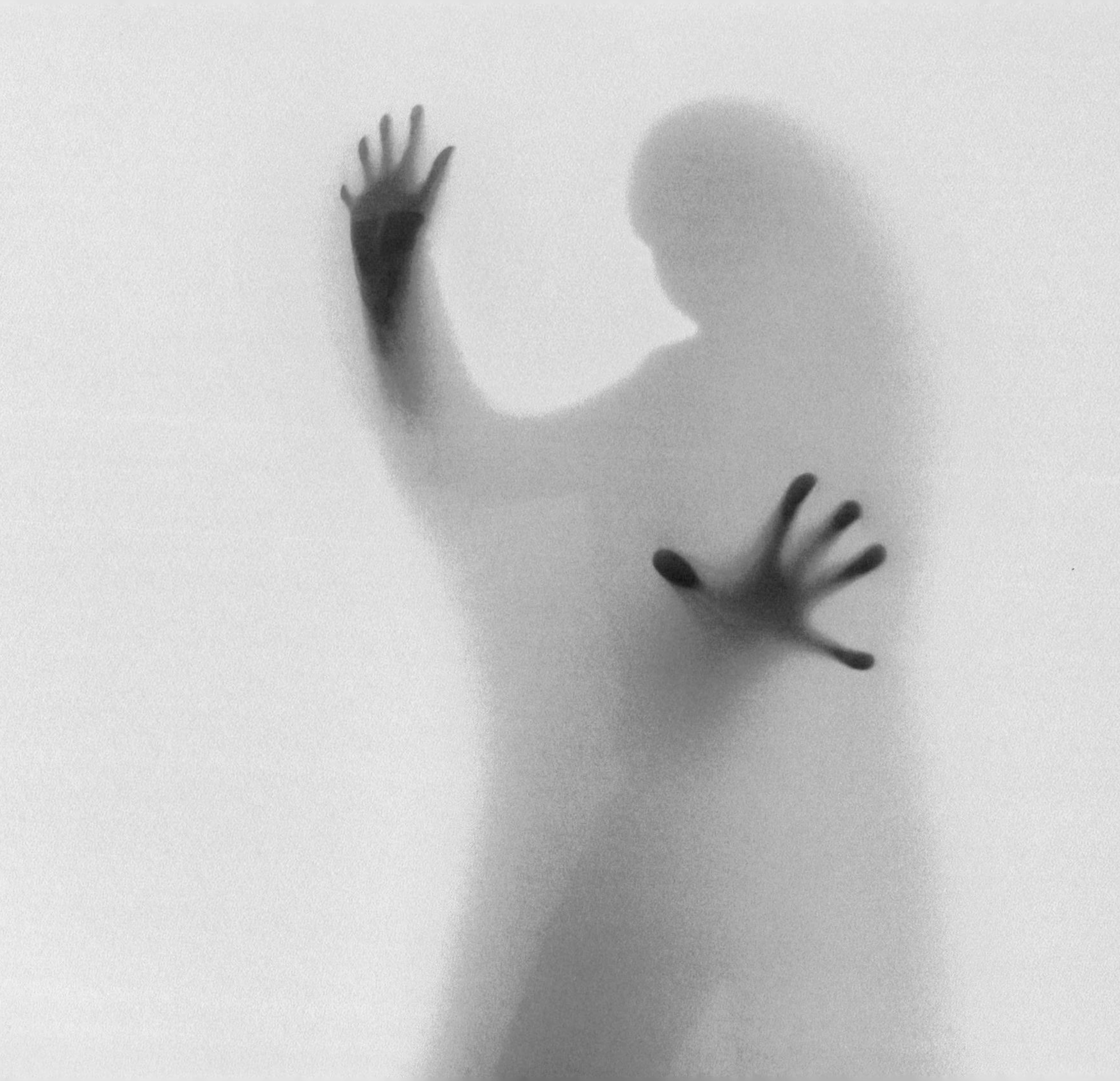

«und die rolle des designers in diesem prozeß? gibt er die richtung für alle am prozeß beteiligten vor?» – «es geht ganz grundlegend darum, allen beteiligten bewußt zu machen, daß sie zu einem prozeß beitragen, dessen ergebnis für jemanden auf der anderen seite sichtbar wird.» – «so, wie die besucher durch den schmalen gelben gang laufen, als ob sie ihren individuellen entwurfsprozeß durchliefen?» – «wer sich durch den gang bewegt, dehnt mit den schultern oder den armen den stoff aus. der besucher weiß nicht, daß jemand auf der anderen seite der gelben wand steht, denn das publikum ist nicht sichtbar. die wahrnehmung, die er bei seinen zuschauern hervorruft, entsteht unbeabsichtigt.» – «ein zufällig aufeinander bezogenes handeln.»

«What about the designer's role in that process? Are you saying that the designer's part is to direct what all these many participants do?» – «It's basically making them aware of that they are actually in a process of something that is visible to someone on the other side.» – «Like the visitors walking through the narrow yellow passage, as if they were moving through their own individual design process?» – «The people moving through the passage stretch the material with their arms or shoulders. Without knowing that there is someone on the other side of the yellow wall: The audience is invisible. The perception of the people watching it develops unintenionally.» – «A random interaction.»

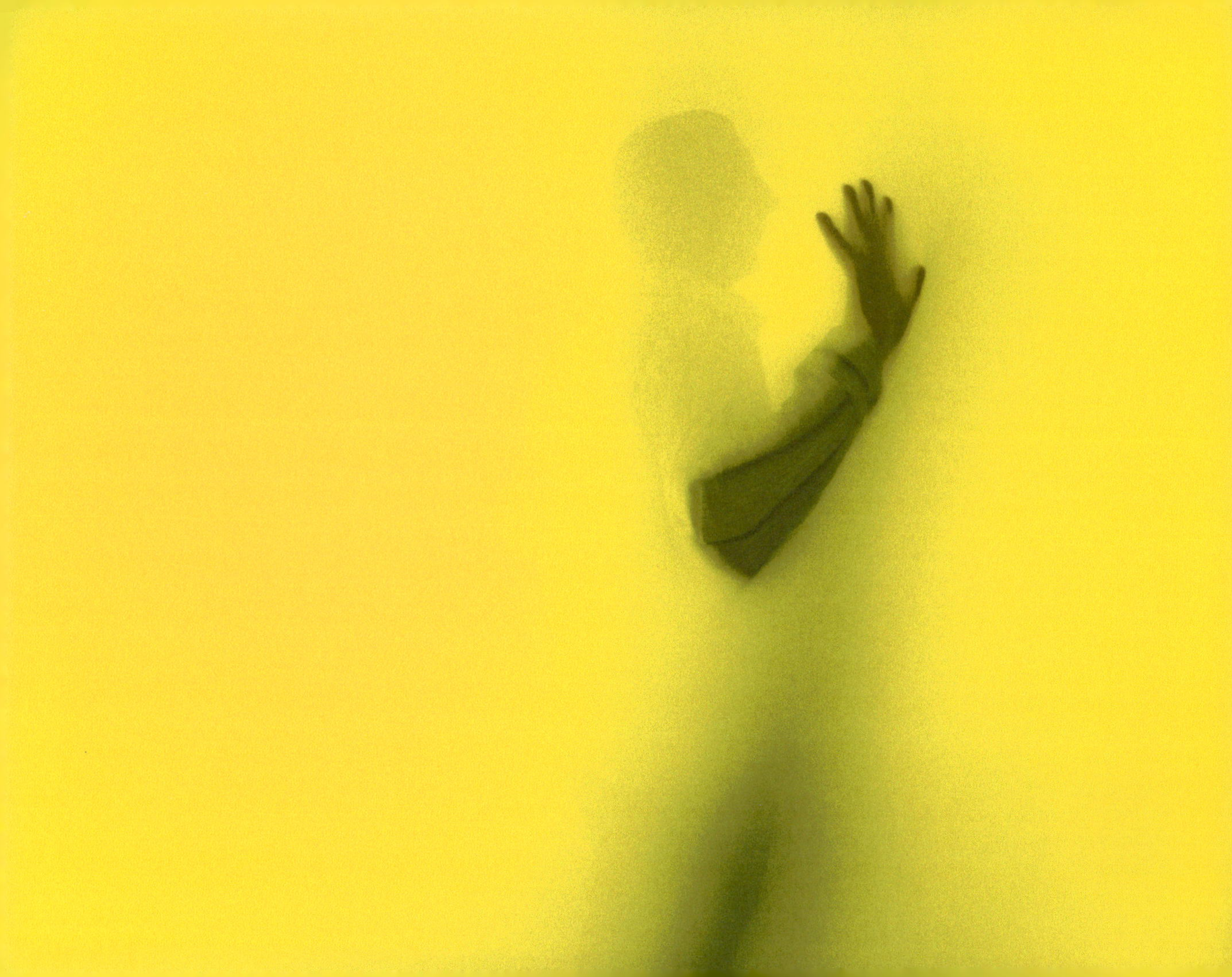

«das ist exakt der punkt: es geht darum, sein publikum und sein medium zu verstehen, selbst wenn man so einfache dinge herstellt wie schrauben oder stifte.» – «erst wenn der besucher, der designer am ende des weges die passage verläßt, gleichsam am ziel des entwurfs angekommen, sieht er das publikum und erkennt, welch einzigartige erscheinung er soeben erzeugt hat.» – «wenn er jetzt eine zweite runde dreht, wird er sich dessen bewußt sein, daß er beobachtet und beurteilt wird. das medium, die schraube oder der stift, kann nicht sehen, aber es kommuniziert.» – «dies ist eine der grundideen des entwurfs?» – «es geht darum, klug auf ein ziel hinzuplanen, worin es auch bestehen mag. es geht um strategie, rahmen, medium.»

«That is exactly the point: Even if you are into basic things like producing screws or pens, it's about understanding the media.» – «Only on exiting from the passage at the end of the journey, having arrived at the goal of the design, does the visitor, the designer, discover the audience and realize what a unique occurance he has just created.» – «If they then went round again, they would be conscious of being watched and criticised. The medium, the screw or the pen, can't see, but it does communicate.» – «Is that one of the basic ideas behind the design?» – «It's about deliberately planning for a goal, whatever it might be. It's about strategy, framework and media.»

von den 684 studien zu designfragen, die im durchschnitt pro jahr in den vergangenen 12 jahren veröffentlicht wurden, hat sich keine mit der frage beschäftigt, wieviele designer den käufern ihrer produkte namentlich bekannt sind. es besteht grund zur annahme, daß es sich, bezogen auf die zahl aller artefakte, um zehntel oder hunderstel von promille-anteilen handeln muß. das gilt selbst für sogenannte klassiker von höchst prominenten urhebern. der designer ist nicht identifiziert.

«haben die designer ihre hausaufgaben nicht erledigt? müssen sie ihren markennamen nicht der breiten öffentlichkeit bekanntgeben?» – «ganz im gegenteil, es gibt eine inflation der kommunizierten designernamen. der name des designers ist eine wertlose dreingabe, um eine ware besser abzusetzen. das ist mittlerweile weder handhabbar noch sinnvoll.»

Of the 684 studies on matters of design published on average each year in the past 12 years, none has addressed the question of how many designers' names are known to the purchasers of their products. There are grounds to assume that it must be only tenths or hundredths of thousandths in relation to the total number of artefacts. This even applies to so-called classics from highly prominent studios. The designer is unidentified.

«Haven't the designers done their homework? Should they not make the public at large aware of their brand names?» – «On the contrary, there has been an inflation in communicated designer names, and it's been a gadget to promote a certain product by using a designer name. It has gone beyond practicality or reasonability.»

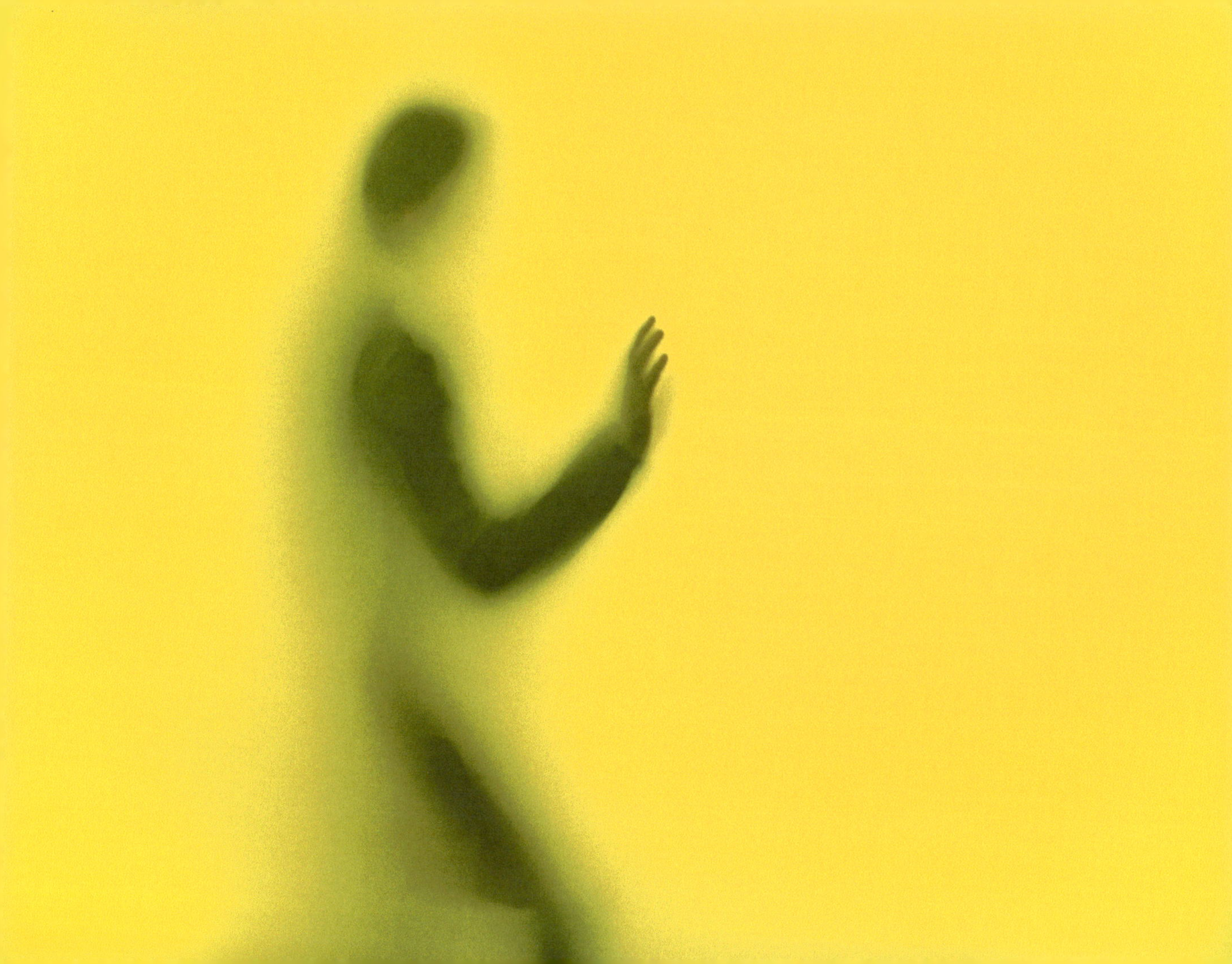

«designer sollten den regeln, die für andere dienstleister und hersteller gelten, nicht folgen? ist das nicht zuviel erwartet?» – «nein. fachwissen sollte wichtiger sein als der eigene markenname. wir sind so fixiert auf medien und bilder, daß wir die eigentliche aufgabe außer acht lassen. ich glaube, daß diejenigen designer für die kommende dekade federführend sein werden, die sich tatsächlich auf den inhalt eines projekts konzentrieren und in die tiefe gehen.»

«Designers should not follow the rules that apply to other service providers and manufacturers – is that not expecting too much?» – «No. Knowledge should be more important than the designer's brand name. We are so media and image related that we forget about the actual purpose. I think that the leading designers of the coming decades will be those who humbly approach a specific design project and go deeply into it.»

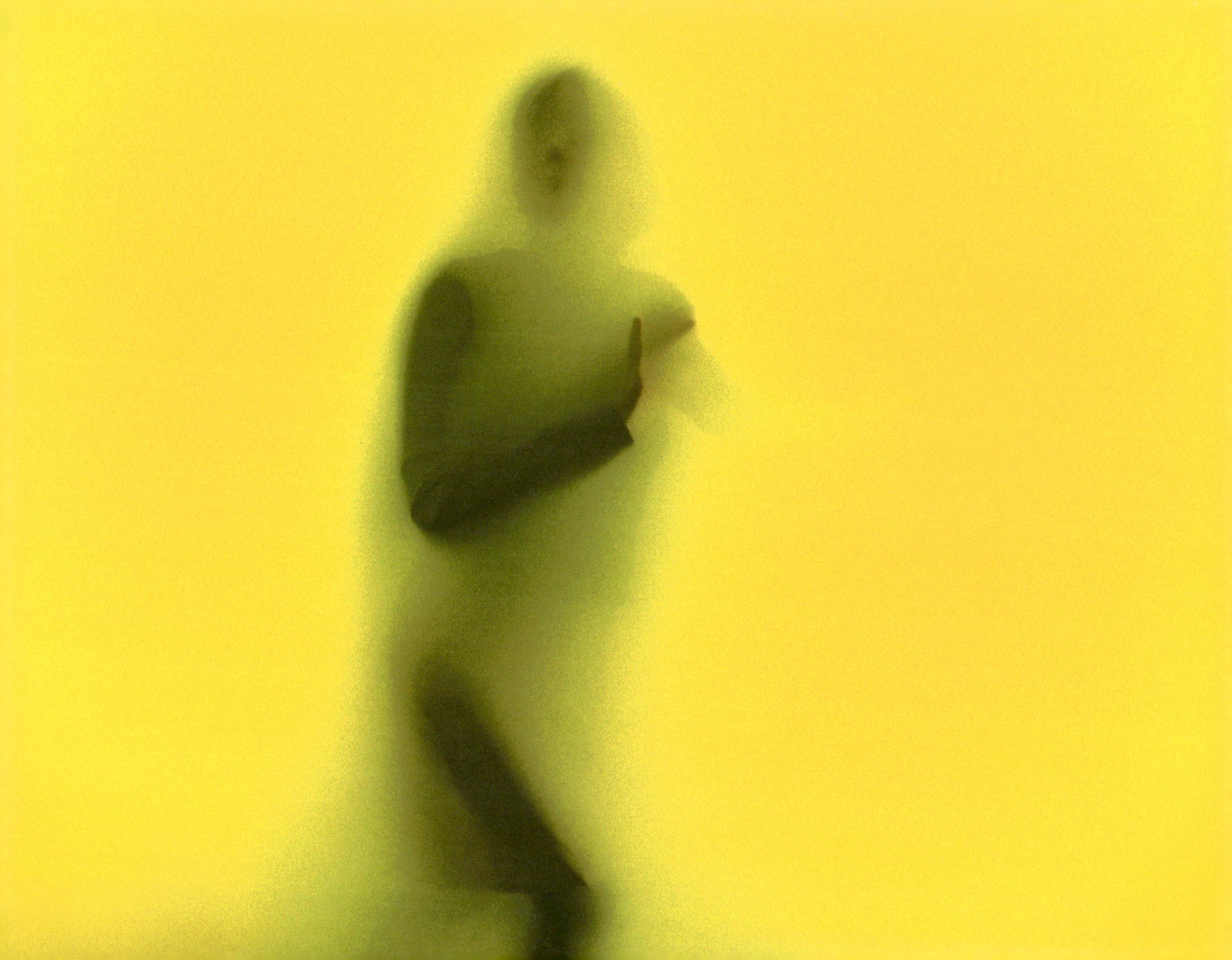

«in letzter zeit wird häufiger ein vergleich zur autorenschaft im literaturbetrieb angestellt.» – «der autor eines literarischen werks muß dieses nicht erst signieren: ein leser, der sich auskennt, benötigt die signatur nicht, um ihn zu identifizieren. der designbetrieb ist dagegen noch unreif. hier übertreibt man, ist zu plump in seinem mitteilungsbedürfnis: ‹sieh her, ich bin es!›»

«Recently, there have been frequent comparisons with authorship of literature.» – «The author of a work of literature does not have to sign it: Readers who know enough do not need the signature to identify him or her. Design on the other hand is still immature: it exaggerates, and is too blunt in communicating: ‹Look, that's me!›»

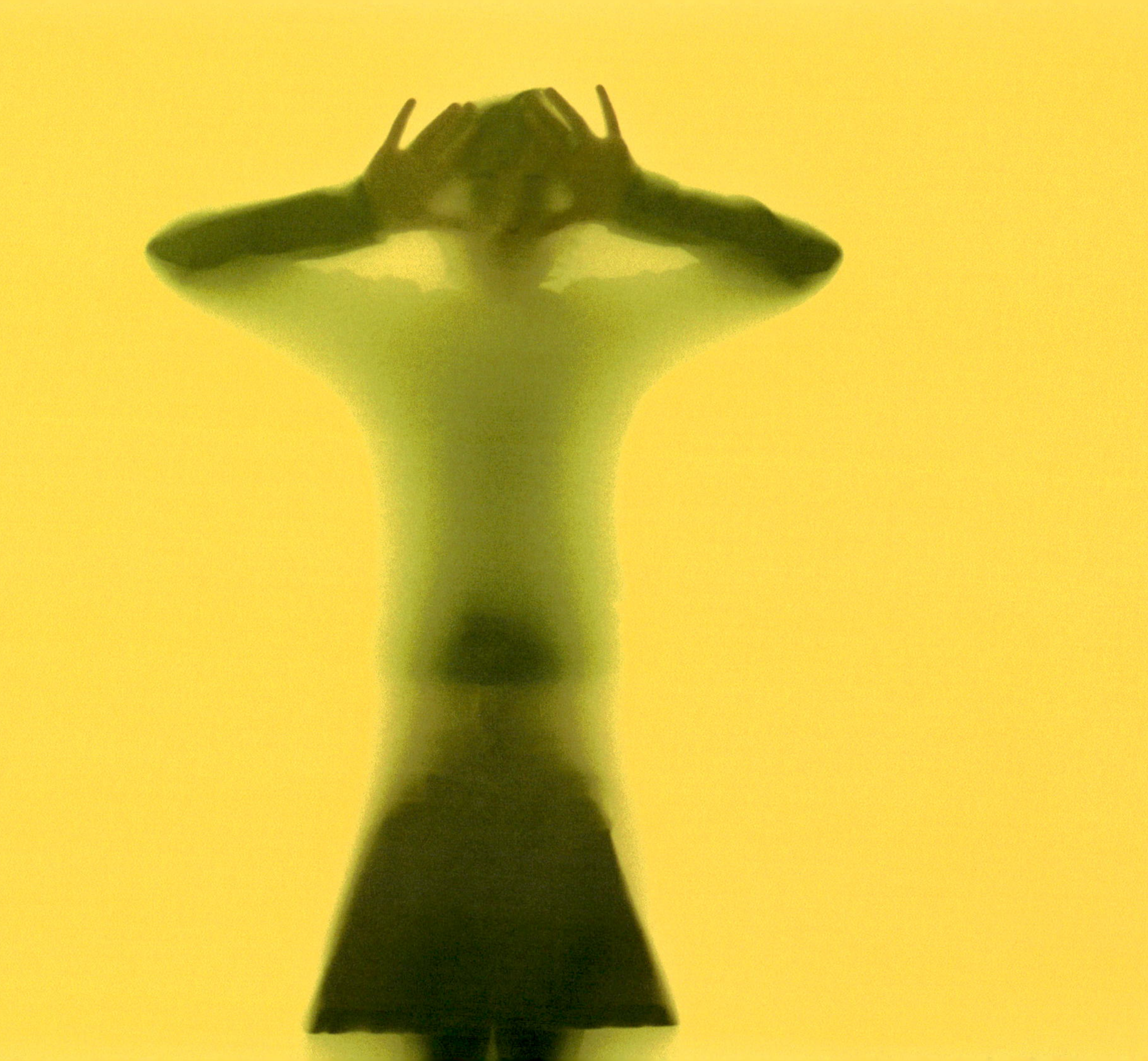

«die installation als parabel auf bescheidenheit beziehungsweise eitelkeit im design?» – «das medium ist die kreative plattform. ich könnte auf meinem weg durch die gelbe passage meinen ellbogen herausdrücken und dabei den kommunikativen effekt erkennen: ‹aha, das bin ich›. daraus könnte ich eine bestimmte art des kommunizierens entwikkeln, eine sprache für dreidimensionale angelegenheiten.» – «gibt es grenzen dieses ausdrucks?» – «selbst wer die wand durchschneidet oder die verspannung verbiegt, macht sich einen namen.»

«The installation as a parable of modesty and vanity in design?» – «The medium is the creative platform. I might be walking through the passage sticking my elbow out and eventually learning to communicate: ‹Hey, that's me›. From that, I could develop a certain way to communicate, a language for three-dimensional aspects.» – «Are there any limits to that form of expression?» – «You could even make a name by cutting the walls or pushing the boundaries out of shape.»

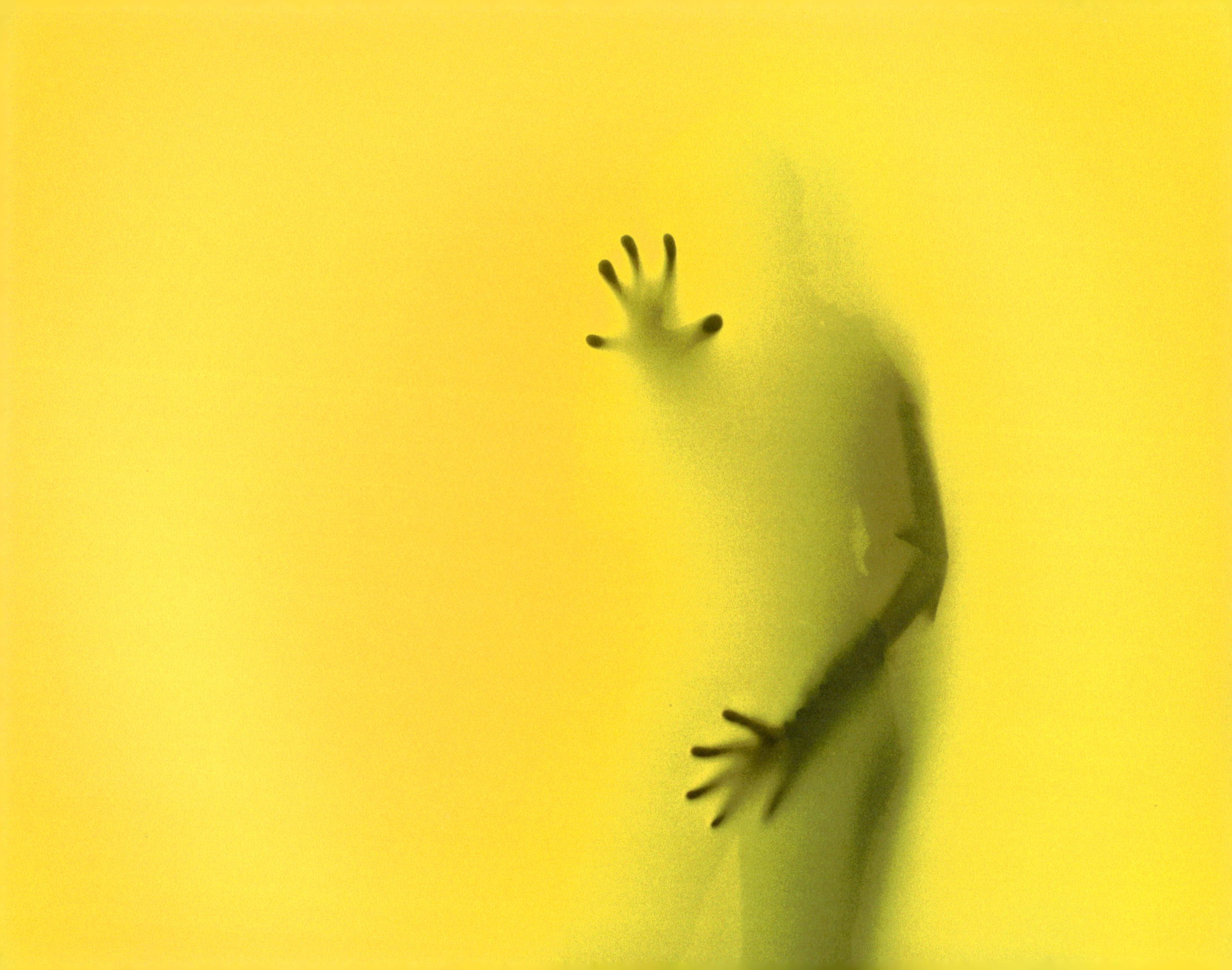

«warum diese profilierungssucht, diese eitelkeit? mangelndes selbstvertrauen?» – «stellt sich selbstvertrauen nicht mit dem erfolg ein? eitelkeit ist eine der wichtigsten antriebsfedern. unsere gesellschaft ist ein jahrmarkt der eitelkeiten. es geht darum, preise zu gewinnen. es geht darum, teil einer erfolgreichen schicht zu sein. identität hat mit eitelkeit zu tun: wen wähle ich zur identifikationsvorlage? viele designer entwickeln ihre identität und ihr profil nach der vorlage eines superstars. aber ist dies hier nicht auch eine installationsreihe der superstars im design?» – «das ist wahr. wir kokettieren beide mit diesem zusammenhang, du als designer und wir als kuratoren. in einer reihe unbekannter hat es keinen sinn, den namen nicht zu nennen. sicherlich wäre es auch denkbar gewesen, für diese wie für die vorherigen installationen unbekannte designer einzuladen. wir kannten aber keine herausragenden unbekannten.»

«Why is there a need to make a name, a need for this vanity? Is it a lack of self-confidence?» – «Doesn't confidence come from success? Vanity is one of the most important accelerators. Our society is a vanity fair. It's about winning awards. It's about being part of a successful class. Identity has something to do with vanity: Who do I choose as a role model? Many designers develop their identity and image by adopting a superstar as a model. But isn't what we have here also a series of installations by the superstars of design?» – «True enough. Both of us are flirting with that context – you as a designer and we as the curators. In a series of unknowns, there would be no point in not naming names. Of course, it would also have been conceivable to invite unknown designers to produce the previous installations. But we didn't know any outstanding unknowns.»

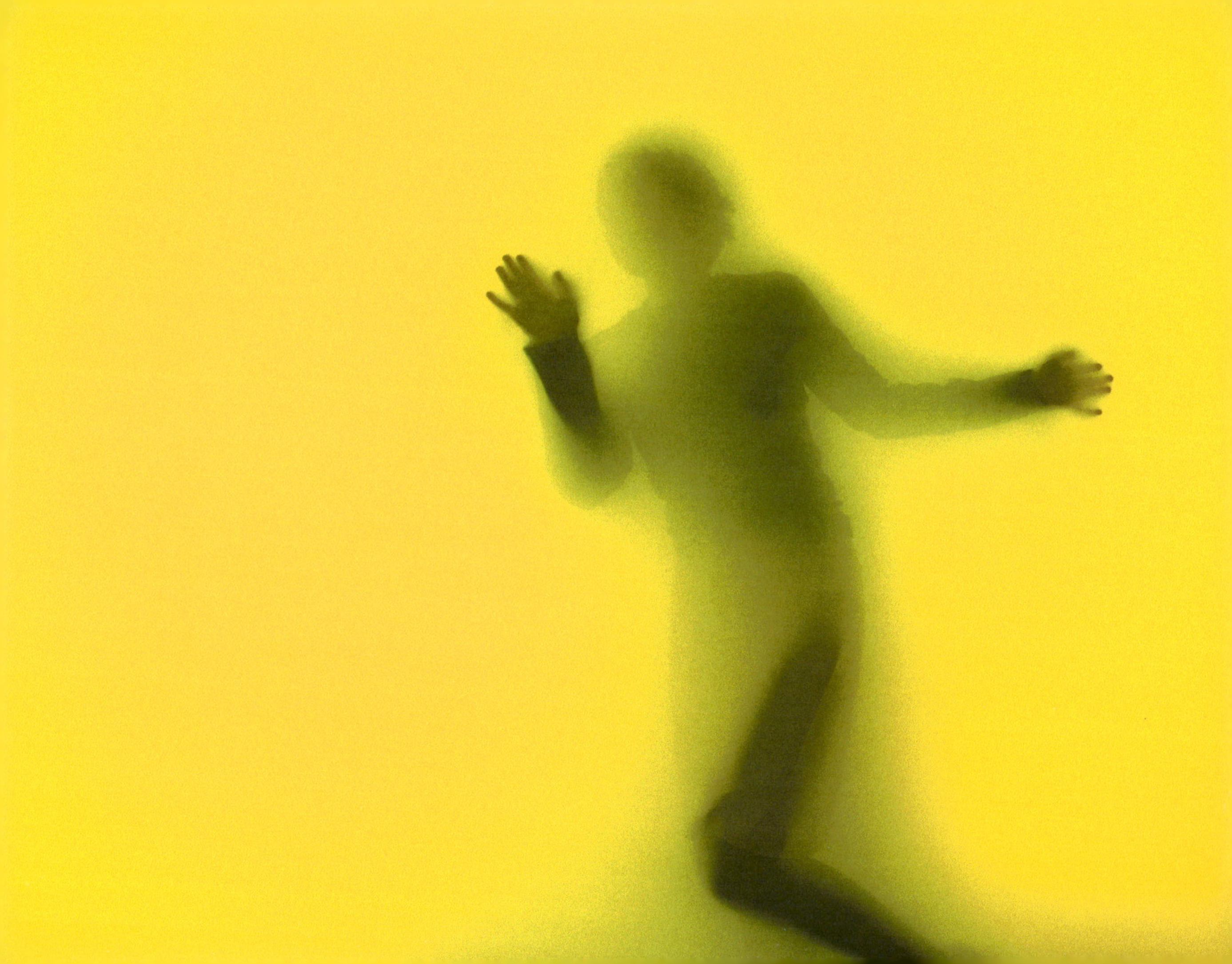

«das vexierspiel ist nicht neu: designer arbeiten für marken, designer werden selbst zur marke, die wiederum von anderen marken genutzt werden.» – «designer sind marken mit einem eigenen lebenszyklus. jeder wird auf seinem weg wahrgenommen, ob er diesen weg gezielt beschreitet oder nicht. wer das nicht begreift, verschleudert seinen wert. es gilt also, sich dessen bewußt zu sein, was eine marke wirklich ausmacht.» – «dann greife ich als markenproduzent doch lieber zum design-superstar.» – «da liegt das risiko.» – «das wäre?» – «zwischen einer marke und dem design besteht ein unterschied. zur zeit werden jedoch die eigenheiten im design so abgeschliffen, daß die erscheinungsweisen stereotyp werden. jeder sieht wie der andere aus, weil immer die selben designer beauftragt werden. am ende ist kein unterschied mehr erkennbar, und das widerspricht der ursprünglichen idee aus sicht der marke.»

«It's by no means a new game. Designers work for brands, and designers themselves become brands which are used by other brands.» – «Designers are brands with their own life-cycles. Everyone is seen on the road, whether they know where they're going or not. If you don't understand that, you are wasting your own value. You have to be conscious of what a brand is really about.» – «So then, as a brand manufacturer, I'm better off going for the superstar designer.» – «That's the risk.» – «What risk?» – «There's a difference between a brand and design. Nowadays, though, the idiosyncratic features in design are being polished down so much that its manifestations are becoming stereotypes. Everything looks the same, because it's always the same designers who are appointed. In the end, there's no longer any perceptible difference, and that is a contradiction of the original idea from the point of view of the brand.»

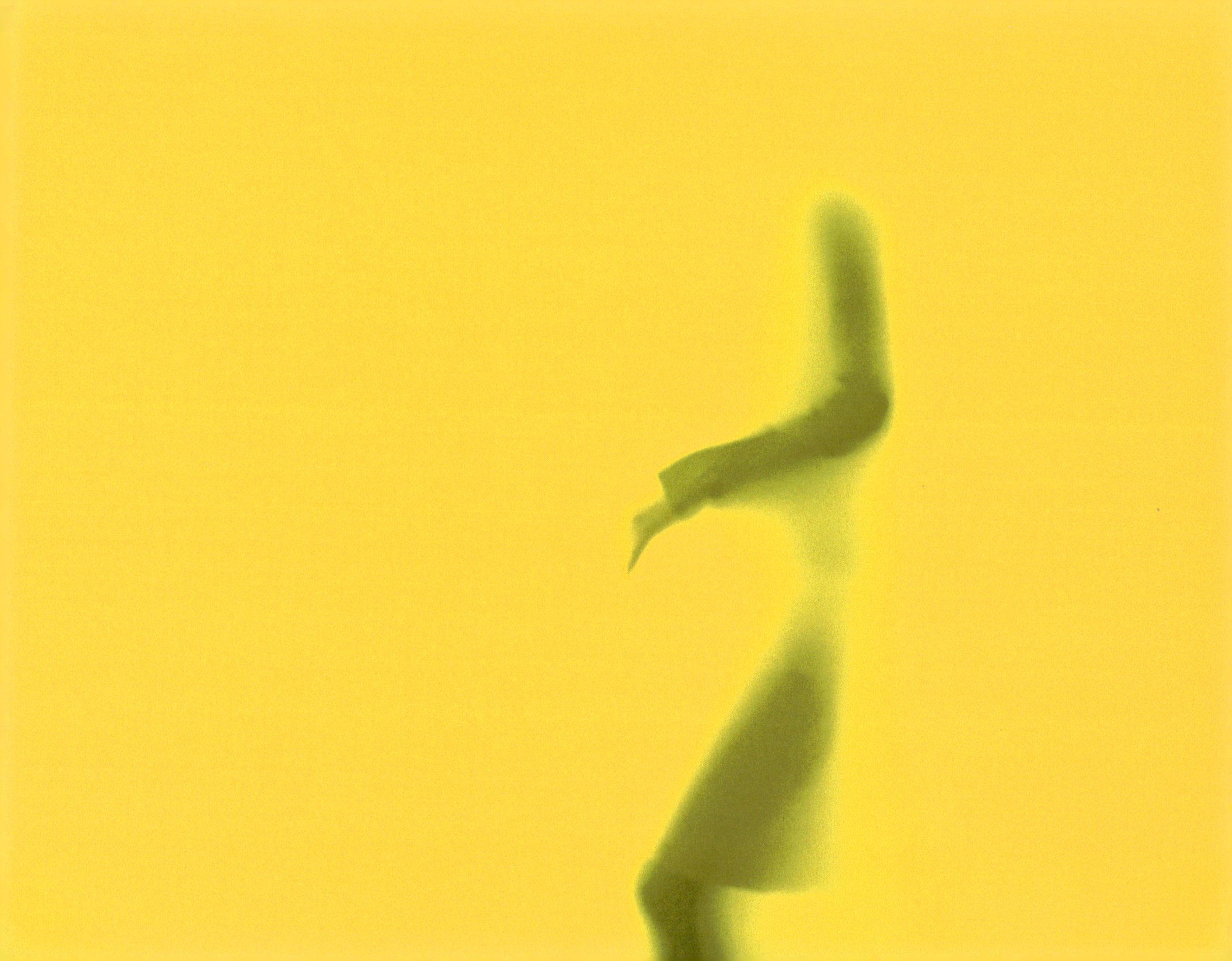

«wenn das aktuelle design stereotyp ist, was ist dann seine typologie?» – «die typologie im zeitgenössischen design ist kein ergebnis eines individuellen schöpferischen talents. das talent besteht darin, in die werkzeugkiste zu greifen. die werkzeugkiste enthält verschiedene typologien, wir können wohl ein paar dutzend werkzeuge identifizieren. es gibt nur sehr wenige erfinder, die ein neues werkzeug hinzufügen. die breite masse bedient sich ihrer und kombiniert sie neu. darin besteht kein ‹was› und ‹warum›, es ist nur styling, auch wenn man damit sehr erfolgreich sein kann.» – «von welchen zahlen müssen wir ausgehen?» – «es gibt vielleicht 20 berühmte designer, die die aktuelle entwicklung anführen. dann nochmals 200 halbwegs berühmte. die unternehmen könnten eine neue qualität erzielen, wenn sie sich nicht immer für die 20 führenden designer entschieden.»

«If contemporary design is stereotypical, what is its typology?» – «The typology of contemporary design is not the consequence of one individual creative talent – it's the talent of using the toolbox. The toolbox contains different typologies. We could probably some dozens tools. There are very few inventors adding new tools. The masses just use them and combine them in different ways. There's no ‹what› or ‹why› about that, it's merely styling, even if you can be highly successful with that.» – «What sort of numbers are involved?» – «There are perhaps 20 famous designers that actually lead the current developments. Then there are another 200 who are semi-famous. Companies could achieve a new quality if they didn't just draw on the 20 leading designers all the time.»

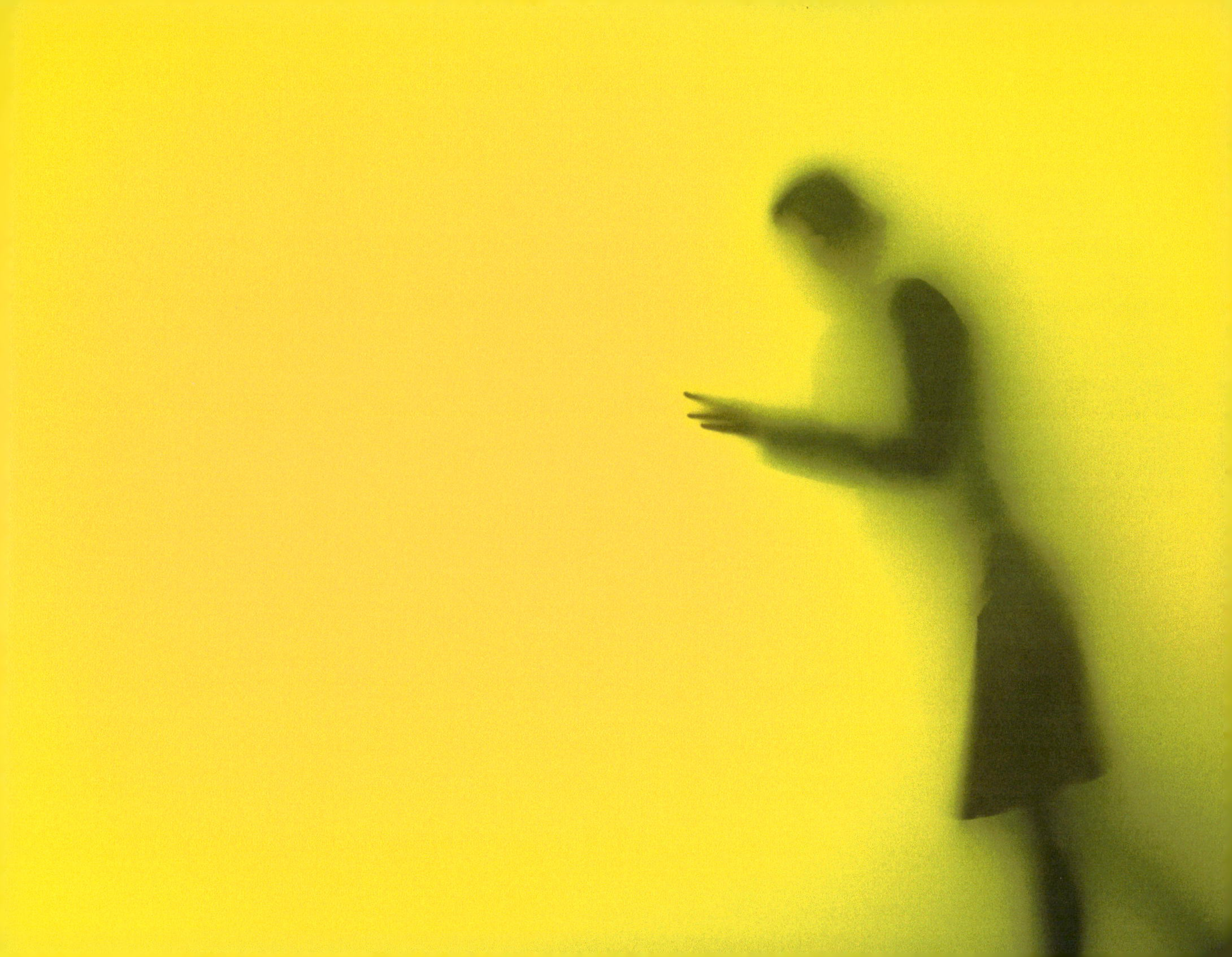

«was geschähe, wenn unternehmen und designer sich von diesem zustand verabschiedeten?» – «die konsumenten haben sich emanzipiert. großes potential besteht darin, etwas neues außerhalb der typologie zu wagen. die unternehmen glauben jedoch, es sei sicherer, in die eingeschlagene, stromlinienförmige richtung weiterzugehen, die im kollektiv der 25 wichtigsten unternehmen und 20 wichtigsten designer entstanden ist. völlig unnötigerweise verhindern wir die entwicklung größerer unterschiede und dynamik, wenn wir uns nicht trauen, die konsumenten zu überraschen, ihnen neue möglichkeiten anzubieten.» – «dafür müßten wir die konsumenten verstehen.» – «wenn wir die konsumenten verstehen, werden wir erkennen, daß sie unterschiedliche werte schätzen. in dieser unterschiedlichkeit liegen große chancen für unternehmen und designer. das defizit besteht darin, daß sie an ihren konsumenten nicht genug interessiert sind.»

«What would happen if companies and designers acted differently?» – «The consumers are mature these days. There is a great potential in daring to establish something which is not within the typology. Companies think it's safer to walk in this streamline direction that is created simultaneously and collectively by the 25 most important companies and the 20 most important designers. We are unnecessarily hindering the development of diversity and dynamics by not daring to surprise the consumers and provide them with new opportunities.» – «To do that, we would have to understand the consumers.» – «If we understand the consumers, we will see that they value different things. That variety holds out great potential to companies and designers. The downside is that they are not interested enough in their consumers.»

«als ich ein kind war, besuchten meine eltern die vereinigten staaten von amerika. sie brachten exotische sachen mit: einen baseball-handschuh, eine football-kappe, lutscher und andere aufregende dinge, die ich noch nie zuvor gesehen hatte. das passiert heute nicht mehr. allerdings wird die globalisierung früher oder später die regionalen unterschiede verstärken. heute sind regionale eigenständigkeiten auf kunsthandwerk und souvenirs reduziert. in der differenzierung liegt die chance.»

«When I was a kid and my parents went to the U.S., they came back with a load of exotic items: a baseball glove, an American football cap, candy bars and all sorts of amazing stuff that I'd never seen before. That doesn't happen any more. Sooner or later, though, globalisation will promote local differences. Nowadays, local differences are reduced to handicrafts and souvenirs. The opportunity for the future lies in differentiation.»

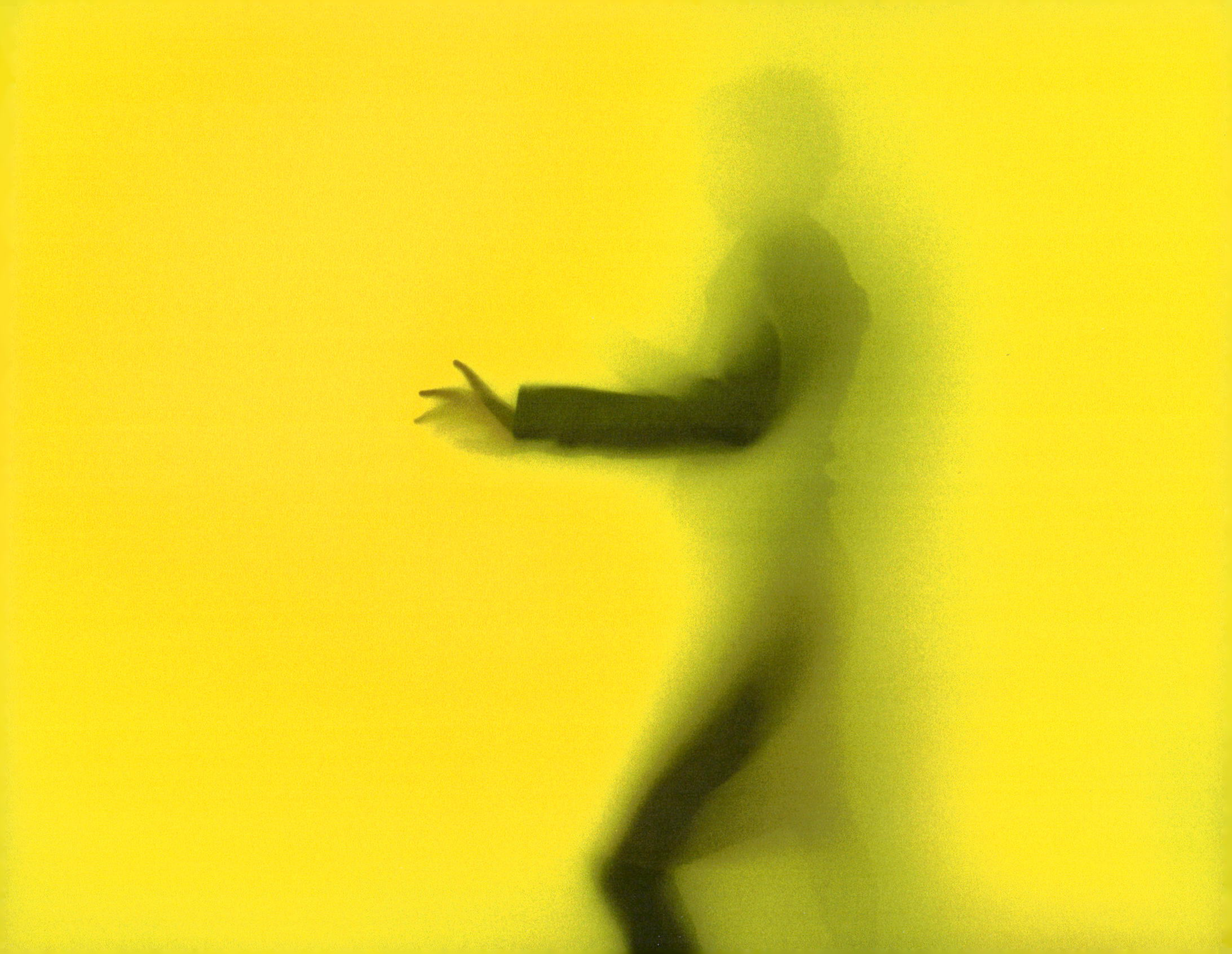

«wenn wir ehrlich sind, braucht der konsument superstars im design. sei es, weil ihm die urteilskraft fehlt, sei es, weil er sich aus eitelkeit mit dem superstar-design schmücken will. was für den konsumenten gut ist, kann für ein unternehmen nicht schlecht sein.» – «der konsument ist unsicher, er braucht einen bezugspunkt, etwas, woran er glauben kann und womit er sich verbindet. aus der sicht des konsumenten ist identität deshalb ebenso wichtig wie aus der sicht des designers. beide müssen sich zu ihrer umgebung in beziehung setzen, und das heißt, beide nehmen am spiel des lebens teil, in dem es darum geht, seine gesellschaftliche position zu bestimmen.»

«If we are honest, the consumers need superstars in design. Perhaps because they lack judgement, or perhaps because they want to bask in superstar design for reasons of vanity. What's good for consumers can't be bad for businesses.» – «Consumers are insecure, they need a point of reference, something to believe in and associate with. Identity is therefore just as important from the consumers' point of view as it is from the designers'. Both of them have to relate to their environment, and that means both of them taking part in the game of life, which is about social positioning.»

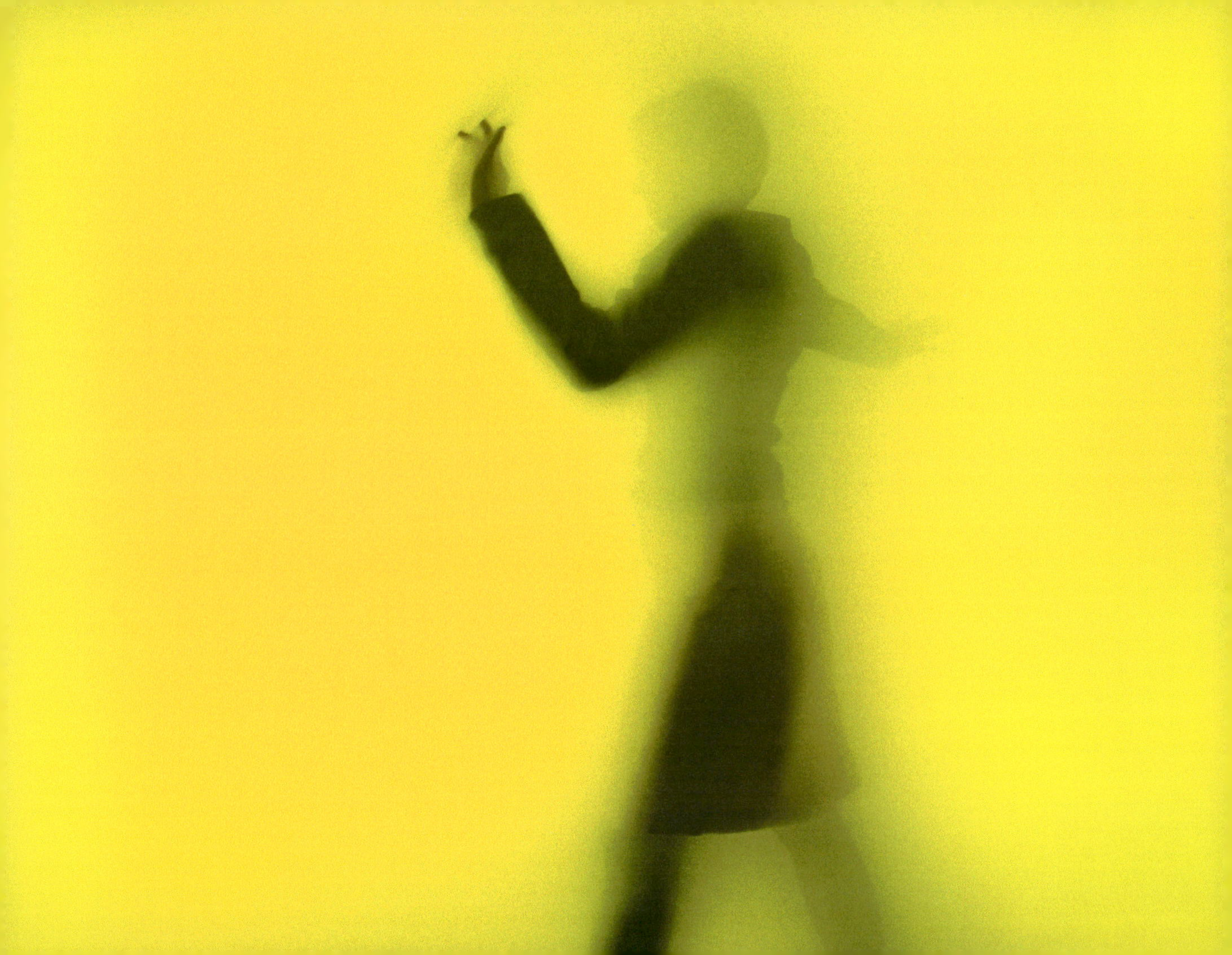

«welchen beitrag leistet die ausbildung des designers dazu?» – «sie vermittelt den jungen menschen, daß das design eine bühne ist, auf der jeder ein superstar sein kann. die designer wären glücklicher dran, wenn sie an ihre aufgabe mit mehr bescheidenheit herangingen und sie von einer breiteren perspektive betrachteten. und wenn sie lernten, daß designer als superstars nur zu einem sehr kleinen teil notwendig sind.» – «die schlußfolgerung für die designer: konzentriert euch auf das medium anstelle darauf, berühmt zu werden?»

«What contribution does design education make?» – «It tells young people that design is a stage where everyone can be a superstar. Designers would be better off if they approached their jobs with more humility and viewed them in a broader perspective, and if they learned that designers as superstars are a very limited part of what is necessary.» – «The conclusion for designers is, then, that they should focus on the medium rather than on becoming famous?»

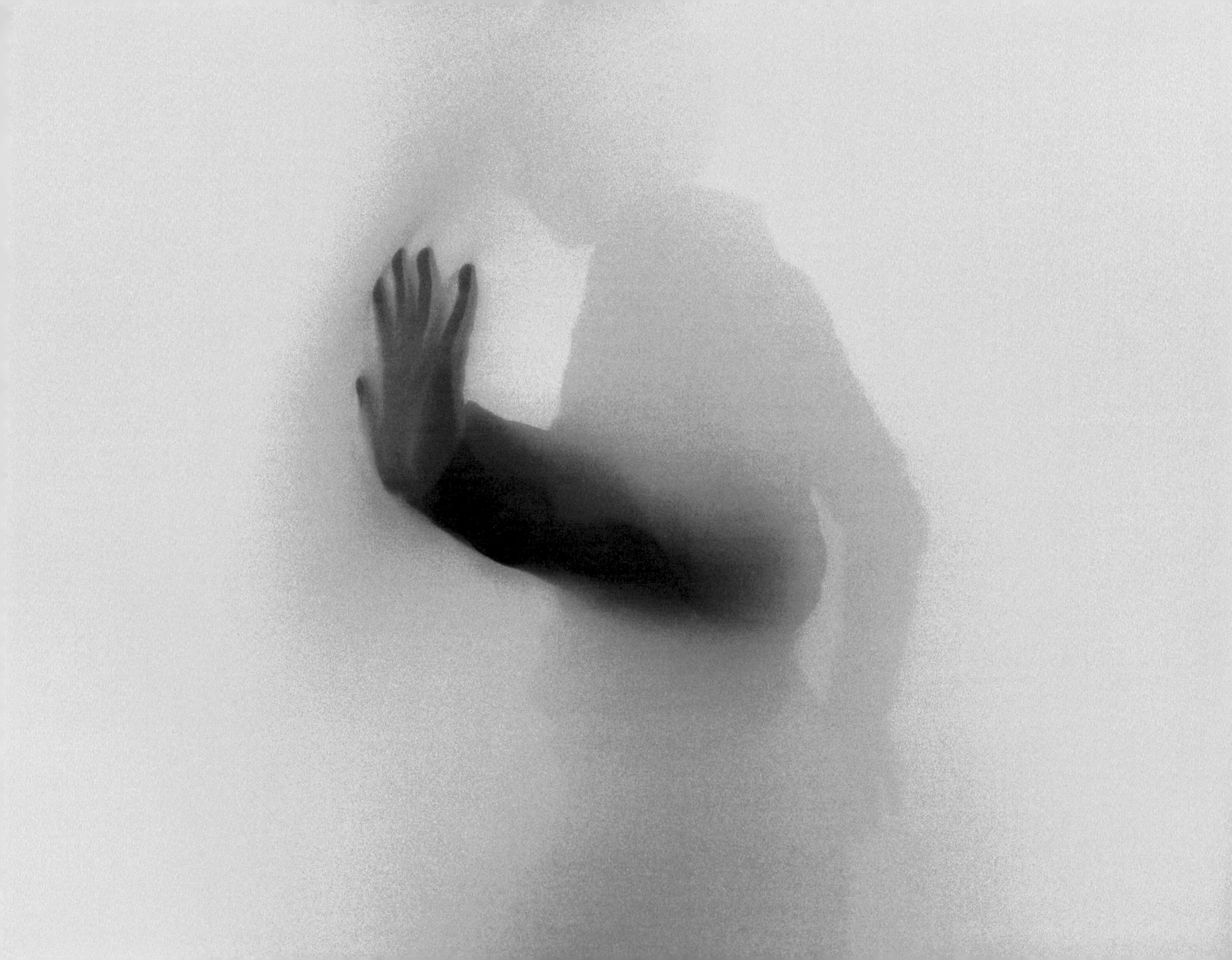

«lassen wir uns nicht von der tatsache verwirren, daß designer, konsument und unternehmensmitarbeiter positionen auf einem dreieck sind, die wechselseitig von den selben menschen eingenommen werden?» – «der designer ist auch konsument. der mitarbeiter im unternehmen ist designer. der konsument ist mitarbeiter. so ist auch der besucher sowohl auf der einen als auch auf der anderen seite der gelben wand zu finden.» – «es öffnet den blick, entzaubert einen mythos.» – «wir haben noch eine vierte position hinzugefügt, die im bermudadreieck des marktes untergegangen ist: die position außerhalb, zum betrachten und realisieren.»

«Let's not get confused by the fact that designers, consumers and corporate workforces are positions on a triangle which are mutually interchangeable?» – «The designer is also a consumer. The employee in a company is a designer. The consumer is an employee. In that respect, the visitors can be located either on one side of the yellow wall or on the other.» – «That opens our eyes and debunks a myth.» – «We have also added a fourth position which had been lost in the Bermuda triangle of the market: the position outside, where you can watch and realise.»

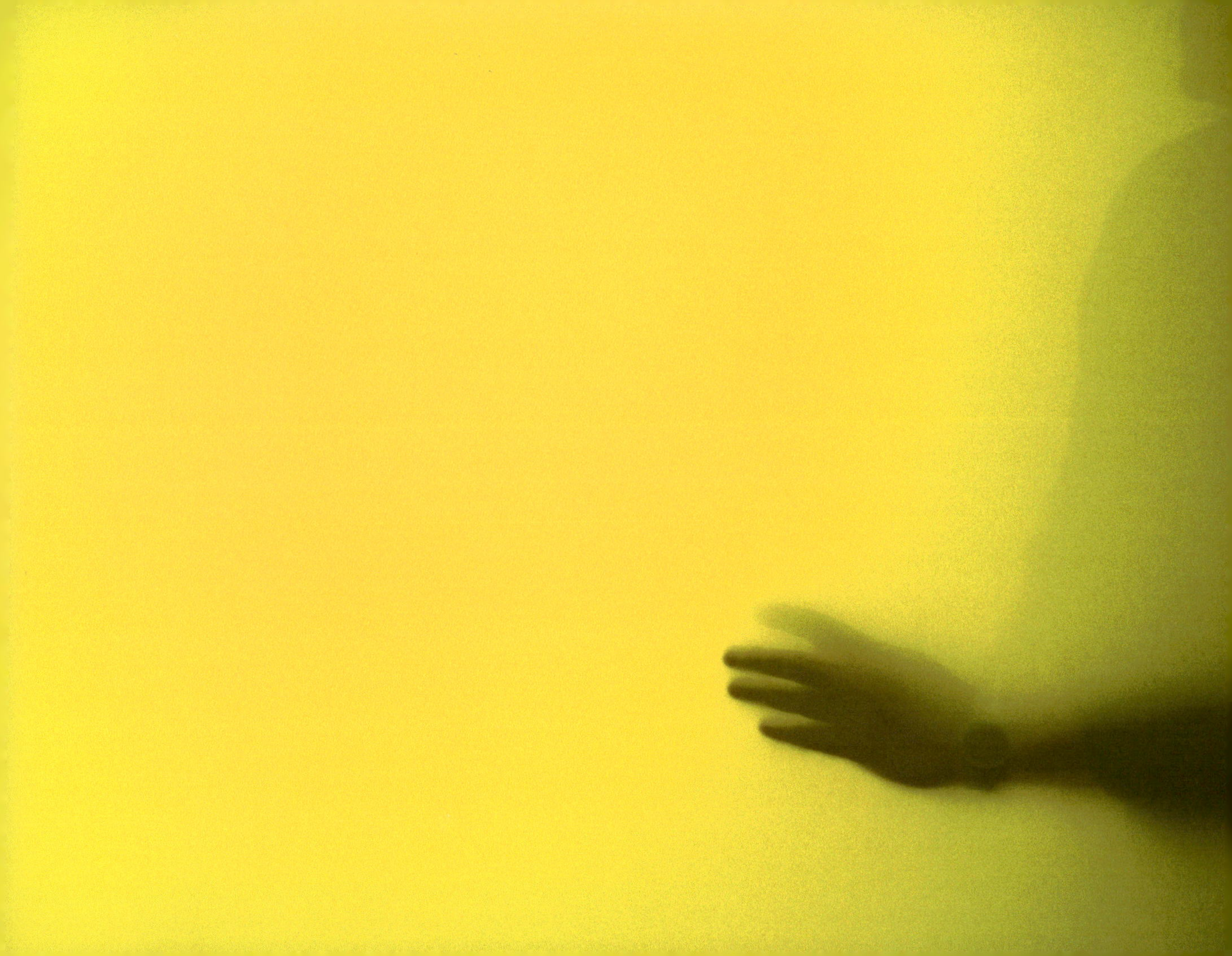

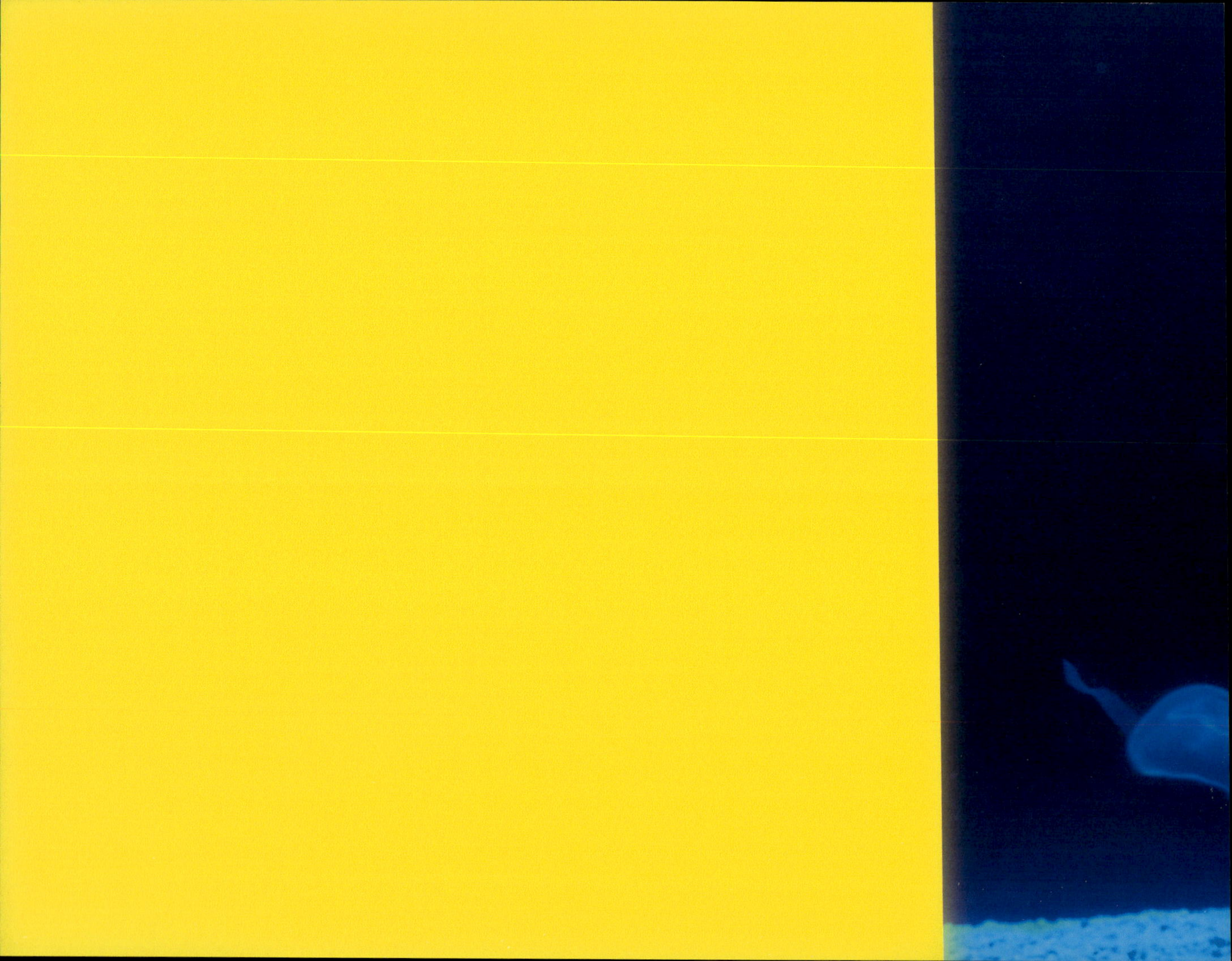

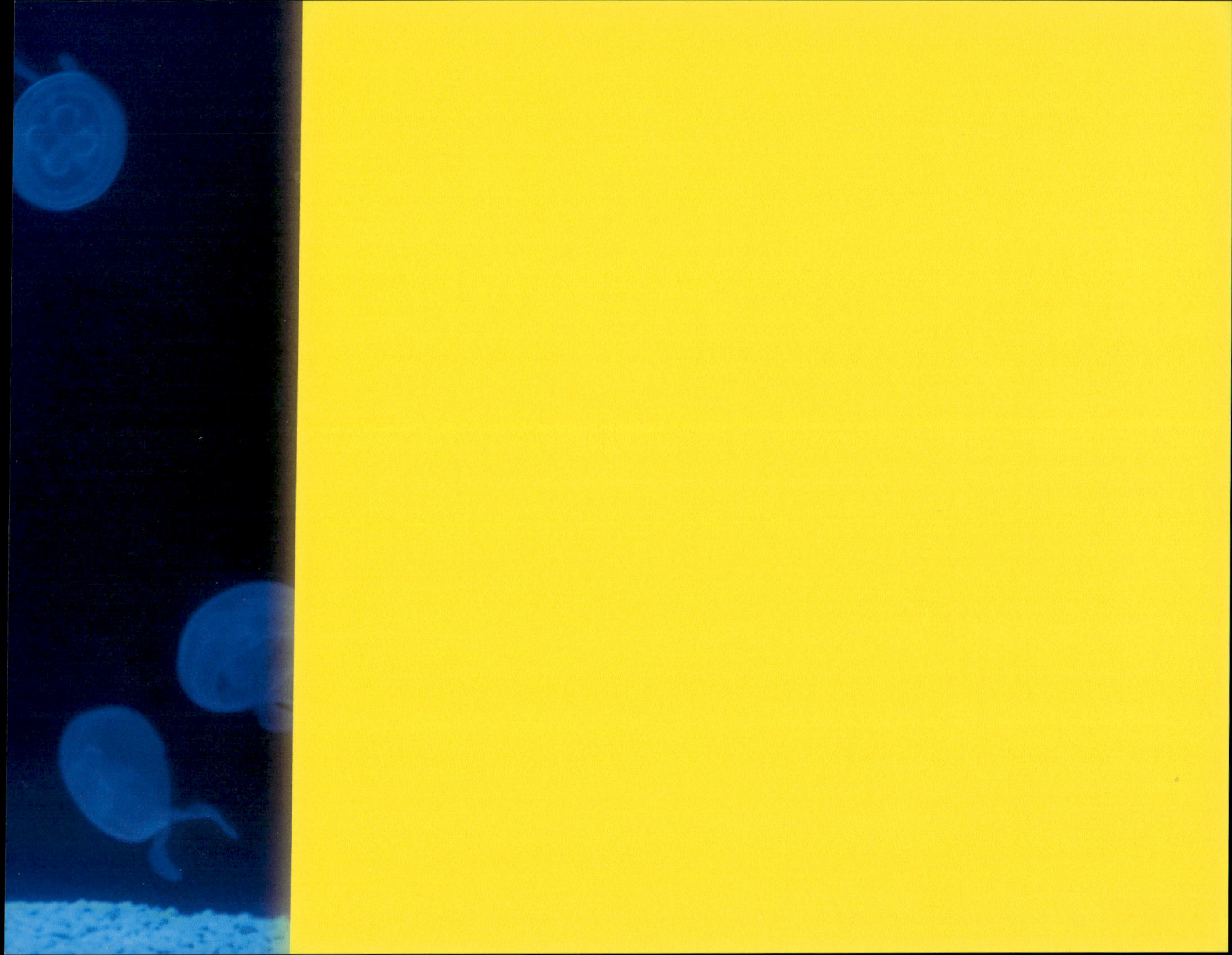

qualle, griechisch: medusa. freischwimmende form der hydrozoen, der klasse von meeresbewohnenden, hohlen nesseltieren mit generationswechsel: der festsitzende polyp als ungeschlechtliche generation und die qualle als die generation, die geschlechtszellen hervorbringt. aus ihren abgeworfenen eiern geht der polyp hervor. sein mit tentakeln bewehrtes mundende schnürt sich ringförmig ab und bildet so durch sprossung eine junge meduse.

Jellyfish (Greek: medusa). Free-swimming form of hydrozoans, the class of hollow marine cnidaria which change sex with progressive generations: the sessile polyp as the sexless generation and the medusa as the generation which produces sex cells. The eggs it lays become polyps. The polyp's mouth end, surrounded by tentacles, constricts in a ring form and buds a young medusa.

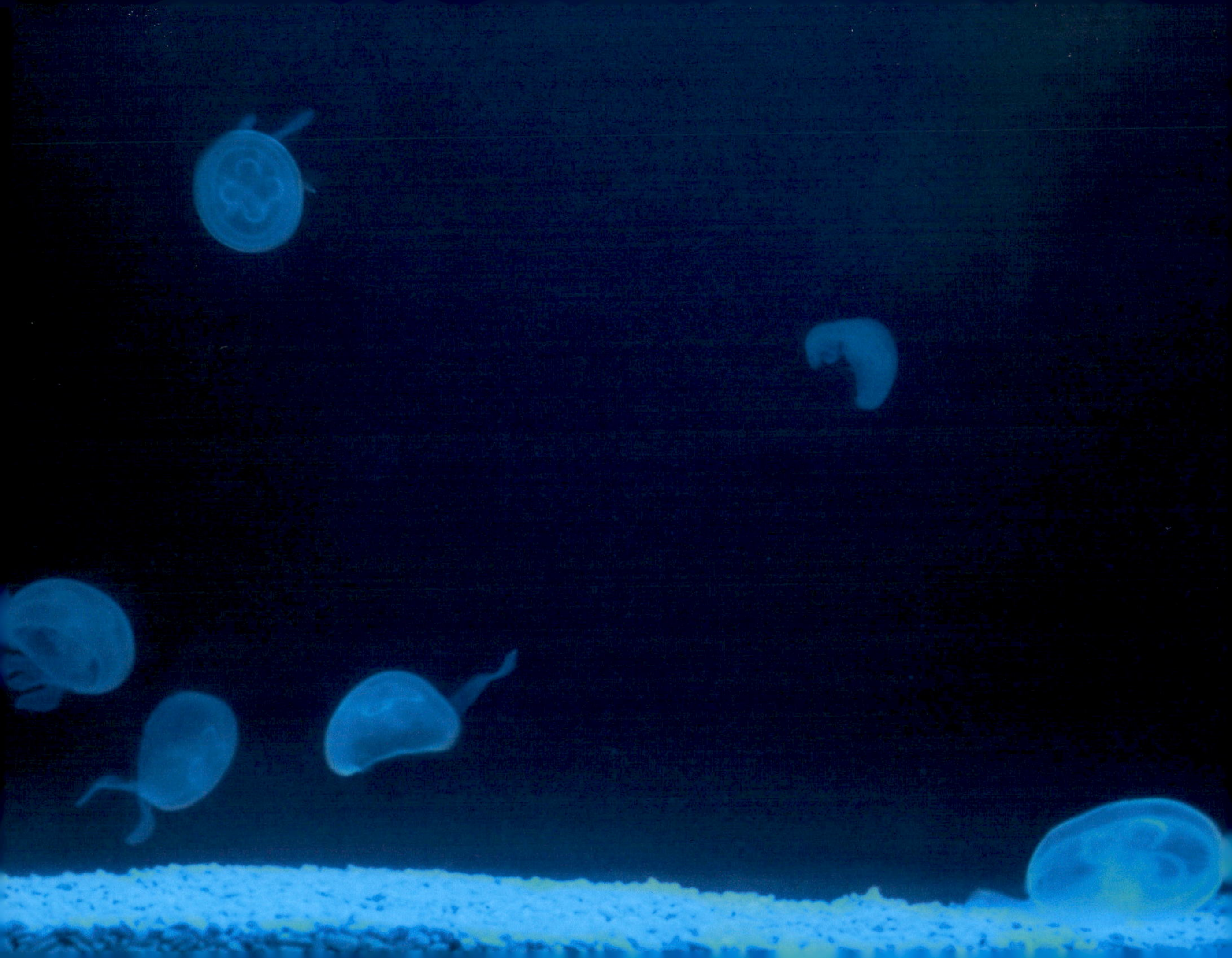

medusa: eine der drei gorgonen, der weiblichen ungeheuer mit schlangenhaaren und grauenvollem haupt. bei ihrem anblick wandelte sich alles zu stein. allein medusa war sterblich, ihre beiden schwesten leben noch heute. perseus, der sohn des zeus und der danae, der mythische gründer mykenes, benötigte die tatkraft von athena und hermes, um das schreckenshaupt der medusa abzuschlagen. seine siegerpose hat sich in unser ikonographisches gedächtnis eingebrannt: breitbeinig, den schlangenkopf mit einer hand schwenkend.

Medusa: One of the three Gorgons, the female monsters with hair of snakes and terrifying countenance. All who looked upon her were turned to stone. Medusa alone of the Gorgons was mortal, and her two sisters are still alive today. Perseus, the son of Zeus and Danaë, the mythical founder of Mycenae, needed the aid of Athena and Hermes to decapitate Medusa. His victory pose is ingrained in our iconographic memory: straddle-legged, swinging the snake-haired head in one hand.

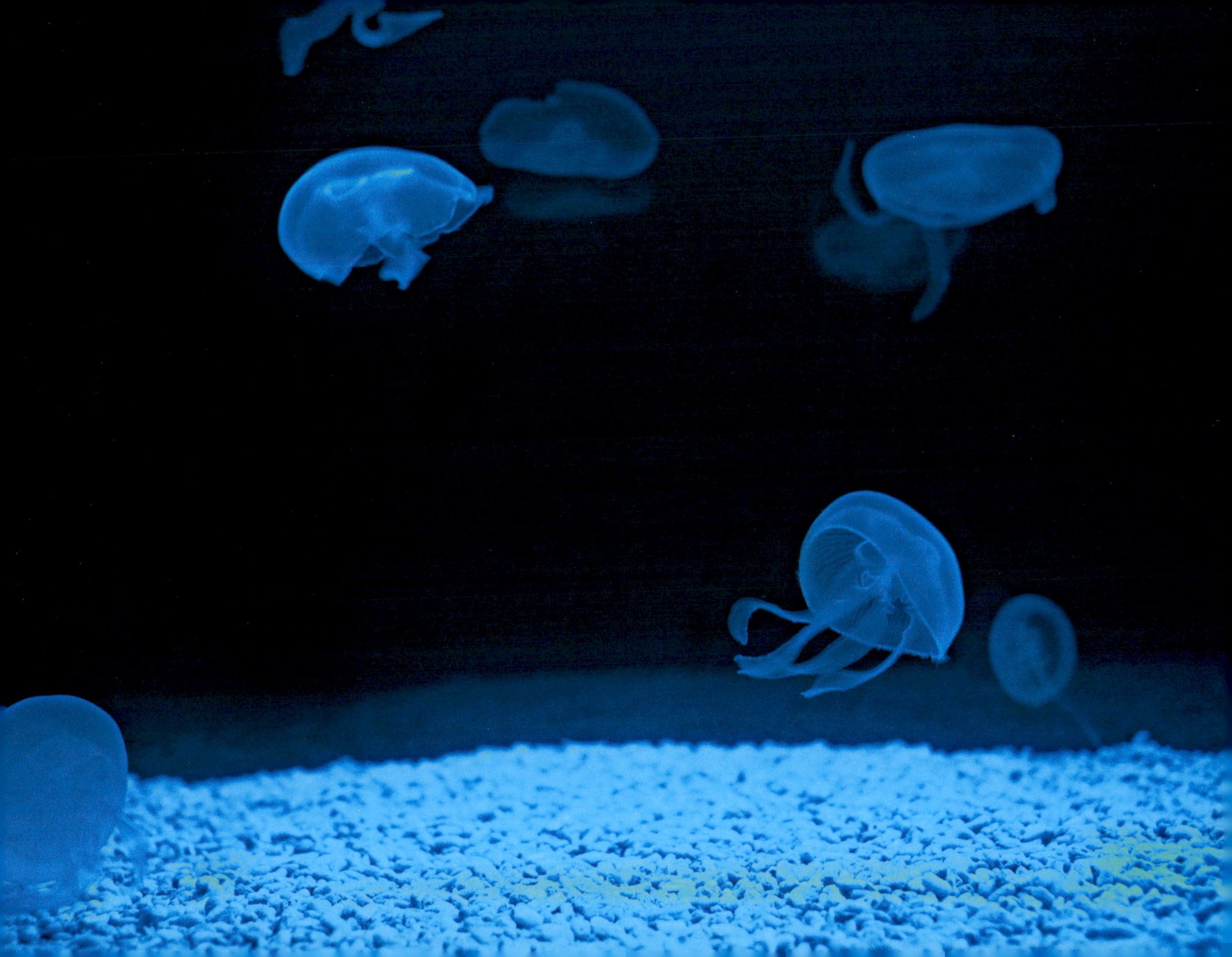

«warum quallen? ein ungefähres ziel der natürlichkeit auf dem weg durch eine passage der künstlichkeit? eine metapher der erstrebten perfektion und faszinierenden schönheit, wie sie letztlich nur die natur hervorbringt?» – «eine mahnung zu demut und bescheidenheit. auch wenn eine tasse etwas bedeuten mag, so müssen wir doch lernen, uns nicht in dinge zu verlieben. mir ist es wichtig, den zustand zu kommentieren, daß wir in vielerlei hinsicht zu opfern der konsumobjekte geworden sind. wir neigen dazu, all das zu vergessen, was sich in der natur befindet und was uns eine viel höhere qualität der erfahrung bietet. das aquarium fügt eine weitere dimension hinzu, die nicht automatisch mit dem konzept verbunden ist.»

«Why jellyfish? A vague destination, the attraction of naturalness on the path through a passage of artificiality? A metaphor for the perfection to which one aspires and the fascinating beauty only nature can ultimately produce?» – «It's a reminder of humbleness towards things. Even though a cup can mean something, we must learn not to fall in love with the objects. It's an important comment on the fact that in many ways, we are being victimised by the objects that we consume and tend to forget about everything that is out there in nature and has an even higher quality of experience. The aquarium adds another dimension which is not automatically associated with the concept.»

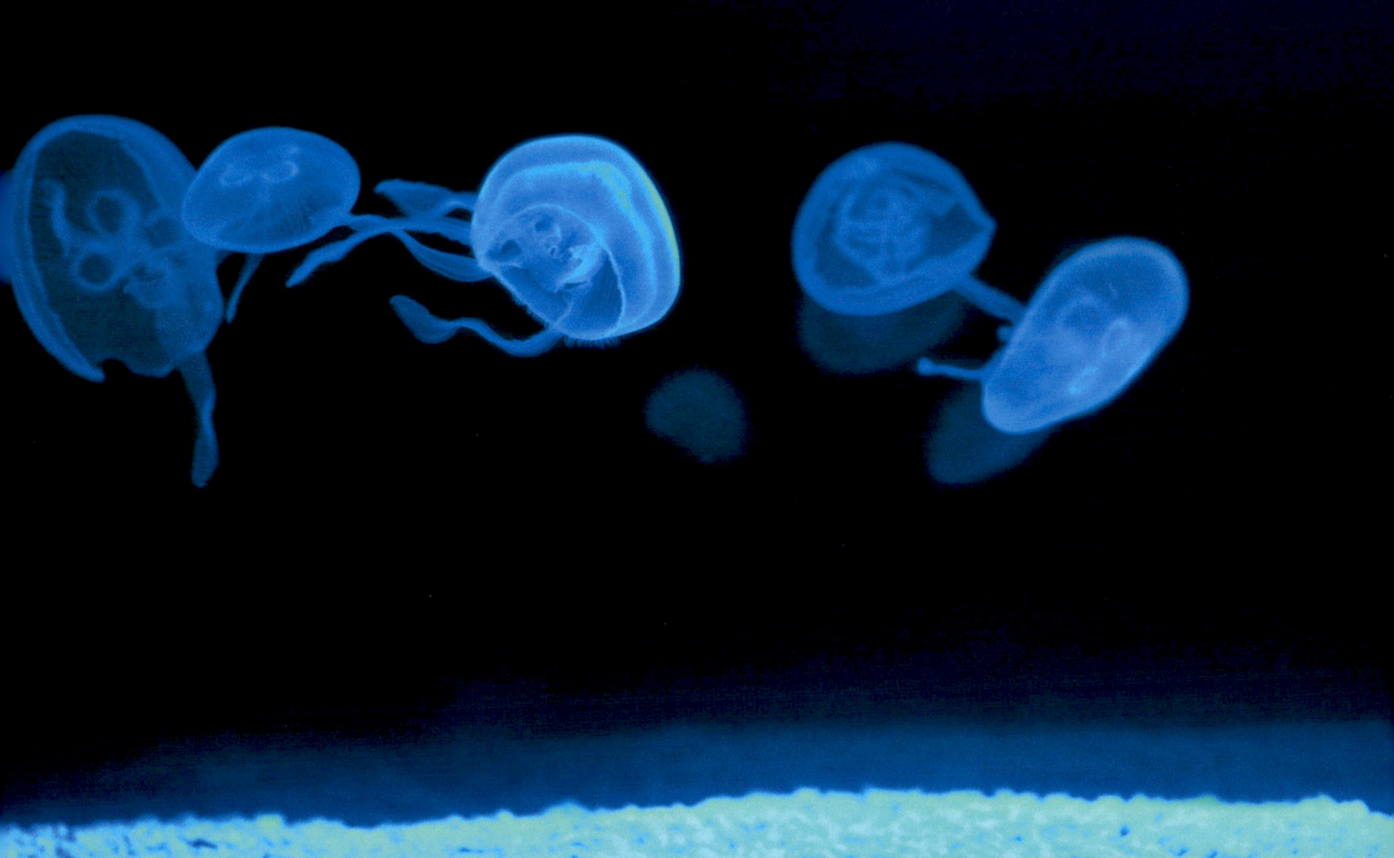

«nimm dir zeit. sieh es dir an. denk nach.»

Take your time. Have a look. Think about it.

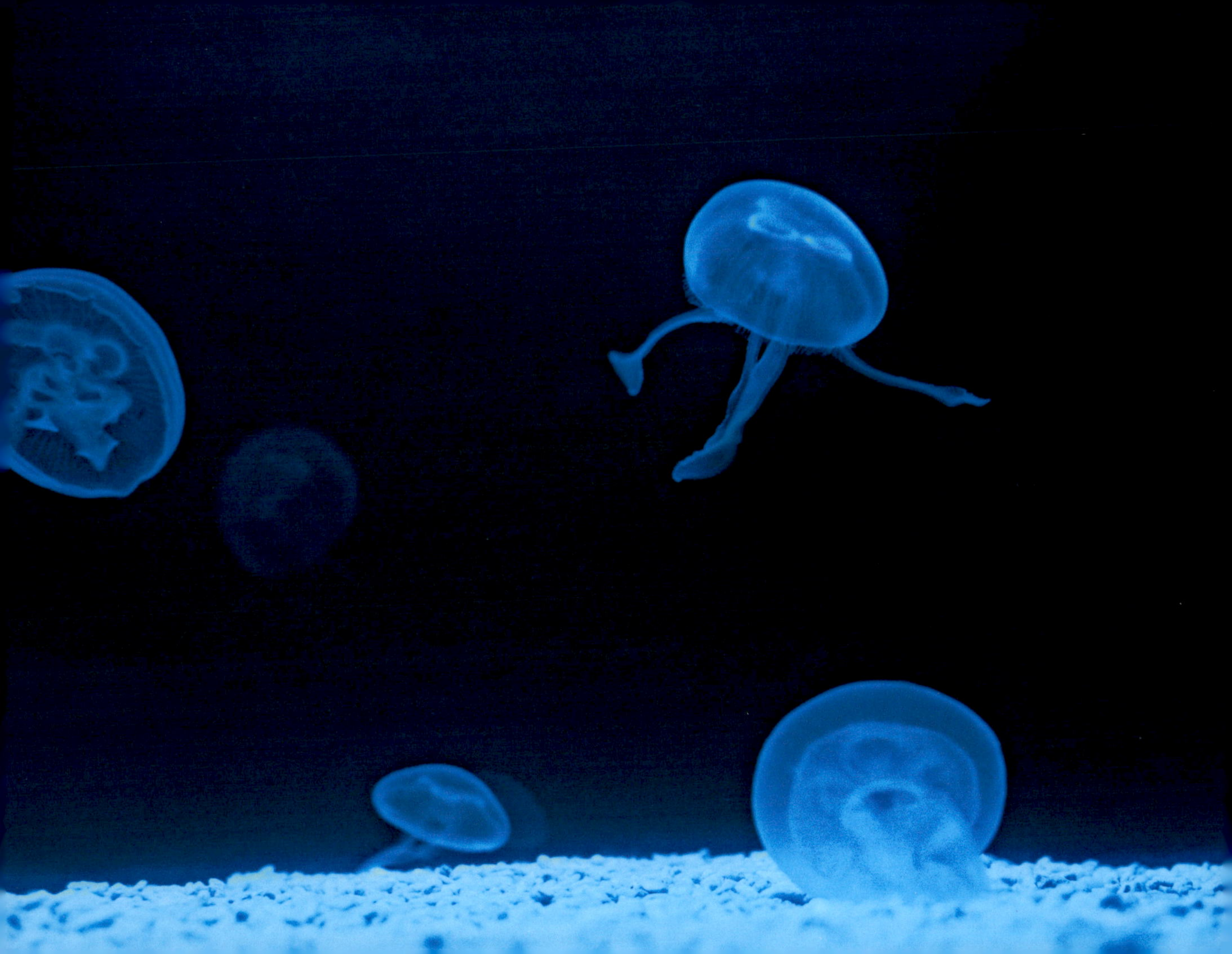

«du steckst in einer geradezu hysterischen situation, alles ist eng und ungewiß, du fühlst dich unsicher, und eigentlich hast du keine ahnung, was geschieht. dann stehst du vor den quallen – das hat etwas kontemplatives.»

«You're in a situation which is apt to provoke hysterics: everything is constricted and uncertain, you feel insecure and you don't really know what is happening. Then you're in front of the jellyfish – there's something contemplative about that.»

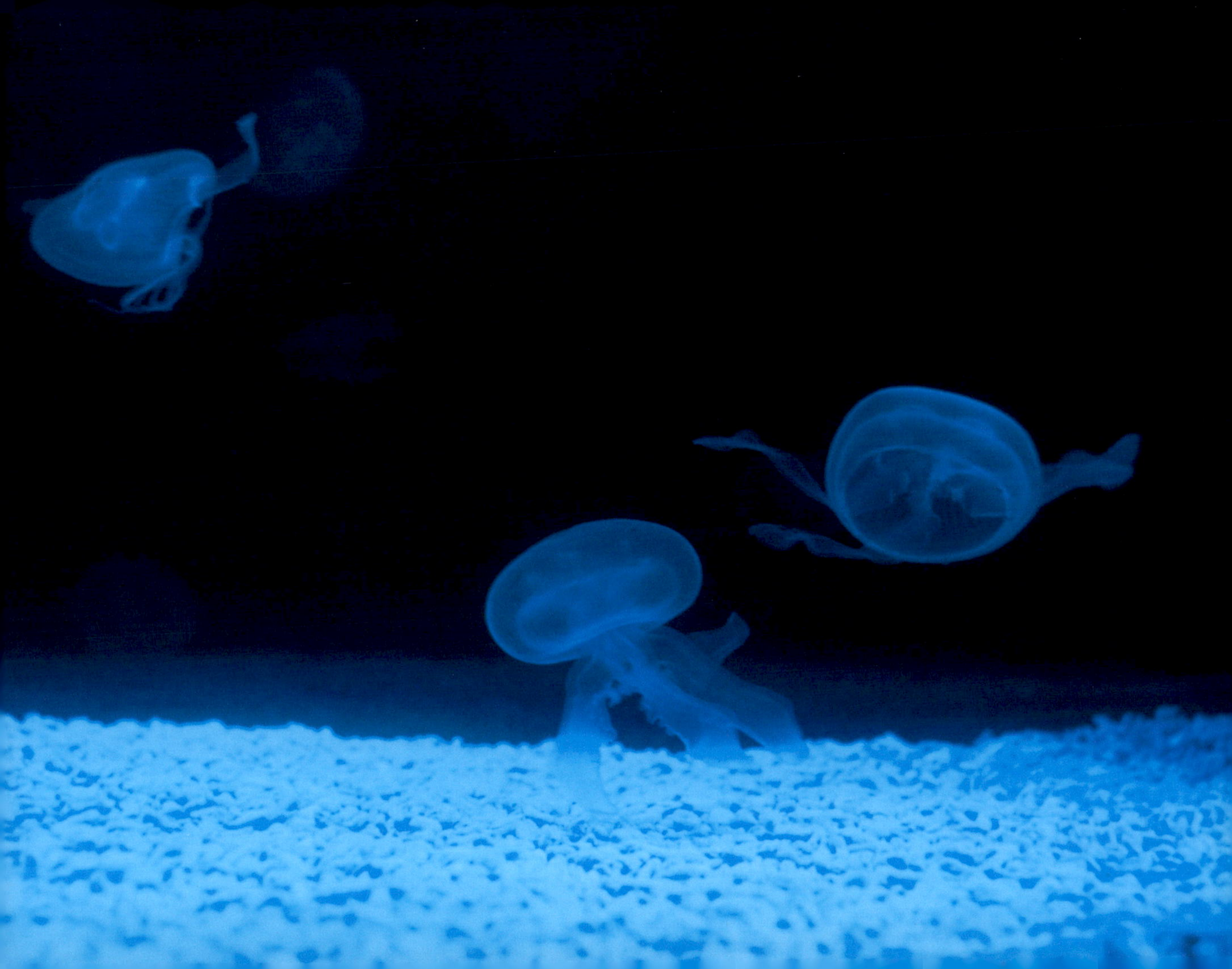

«distanz ist nötig. die quallen gehören hinter glas inszeniert, dort symbolisieren sie harmonie im gegensatz zum mentalen chaos, das ich in der gelben passage erlebe. im meer möchte ich ihnen nicht begegnen.» – «um zwischen chaos und harmonie zu unterscheiden, braucht man distanz?»

«Distance is necessary. The jellyfish belong in their presentation behind glass. There, they symbolise harmony in contrast to the mental chaos I feel in the yellow passage. I wouldn't like to meet them in the sea.» – «Do you need distance to distinguish between chaos and harmony?»

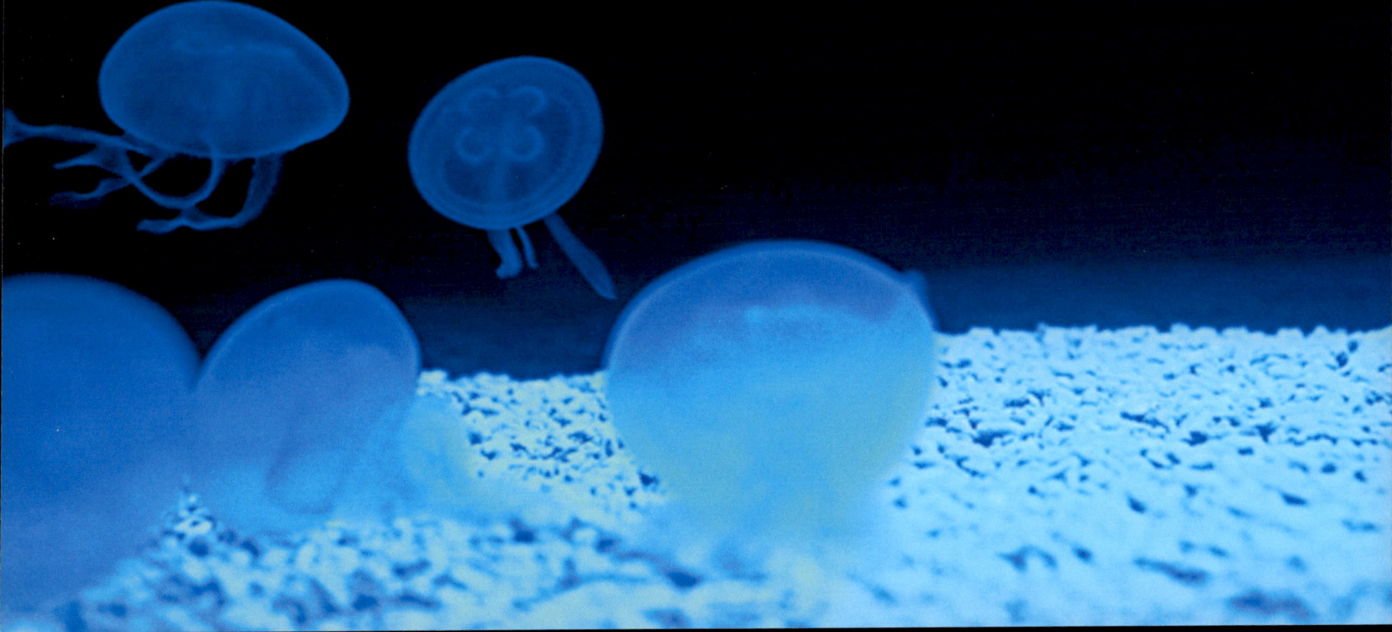

«die quallen als kommentar zu den stilkategorien ‹organisches design› versus ‹funktionalistisches design›?» – «überhaupt nicht. es ist nur eine chance, die den besuchern geboten wird, um nachzudenken. beim ersten entwurf kann nicht alles richtig sein, es geht also darum, den entwurfsprozeß kennenzulernen und ihn danach erneut aufzunehmen. die quallen verlangsamen ihn durch ihre unmittelbar meditative art.» – «ein appell gegen die geschwindigkeit im design?»

«Are the jellyfish a comment on the conflict of styles between ‹organic design› and ‹functional design›?» – «Not at all. It's just a chance to think for the visitors. Not everything can be right in the first draft, so the thing is to get to know the design process and start it again. The jellyfish slow it down with their directly meditative nature.» – «An appeal against speed in design?»

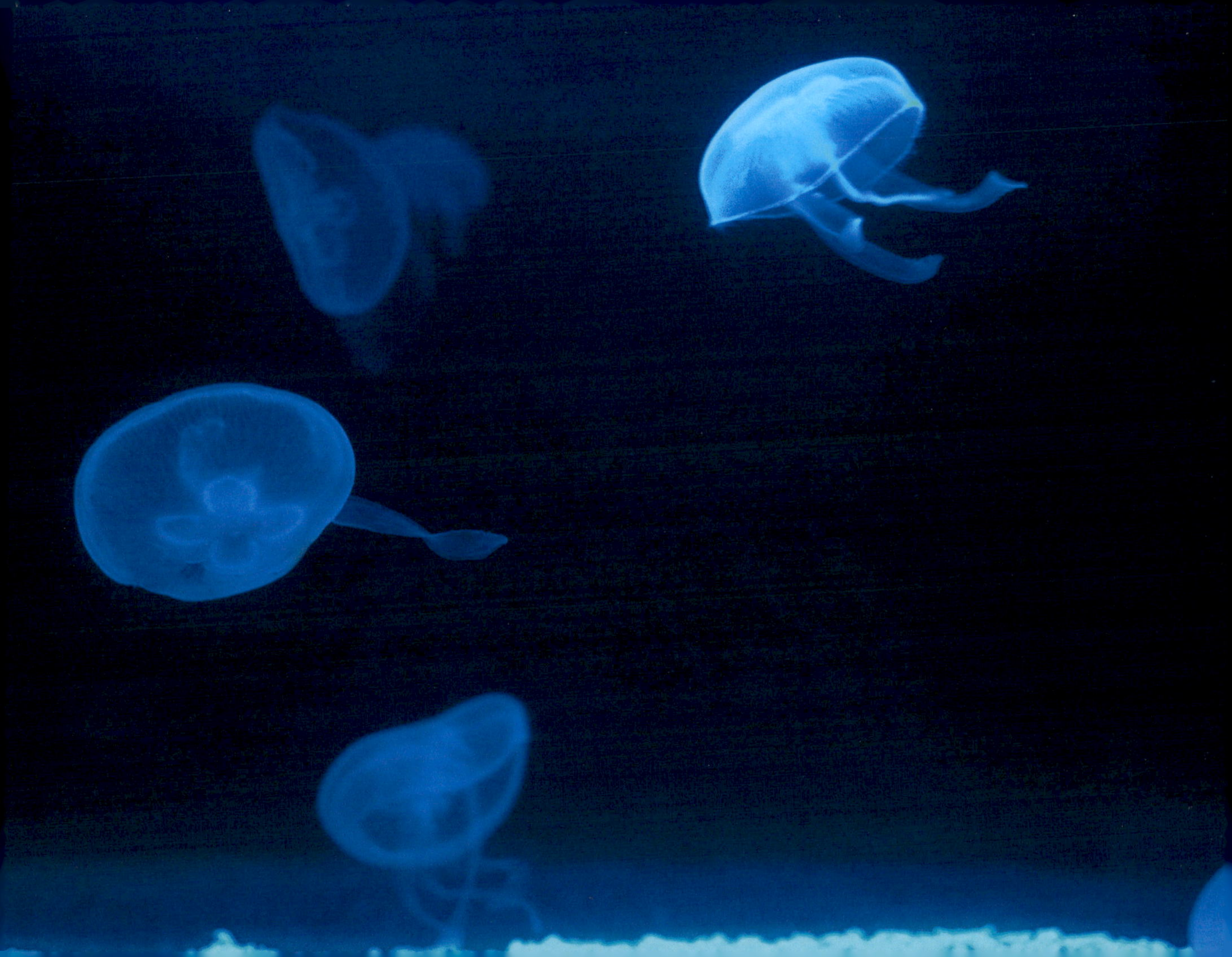

«es läßt sich nicht leugnen: von zeit zu zeit freuen wir uns über eine ästhetische erfrischung. geschwindigkeit ist also teil des designs.» – «dieser gedanke beleuchtet einen anderen aspekt von nachhaltigkeit: wir können objekte praktisch und funktionell nachhaltiger produzieren, indem wir beständigere materialien verwenden und für eine größere haltbarkeit sorgen. aber wie ist es um ästhetische nachhaltigkeit bestellt? das ist eine ganz andere frage.»

«It cannot be denied: from time to time, we enjoy an aesthetic refreshment. So speed is part of design.» – «That idea sheds light on another aspect of sustainability: We can produce objects that are practically and functionally sustainable by using more durable materials and working towards a longer service life. But what about aesthetic sustainability? That's a totally different question.»

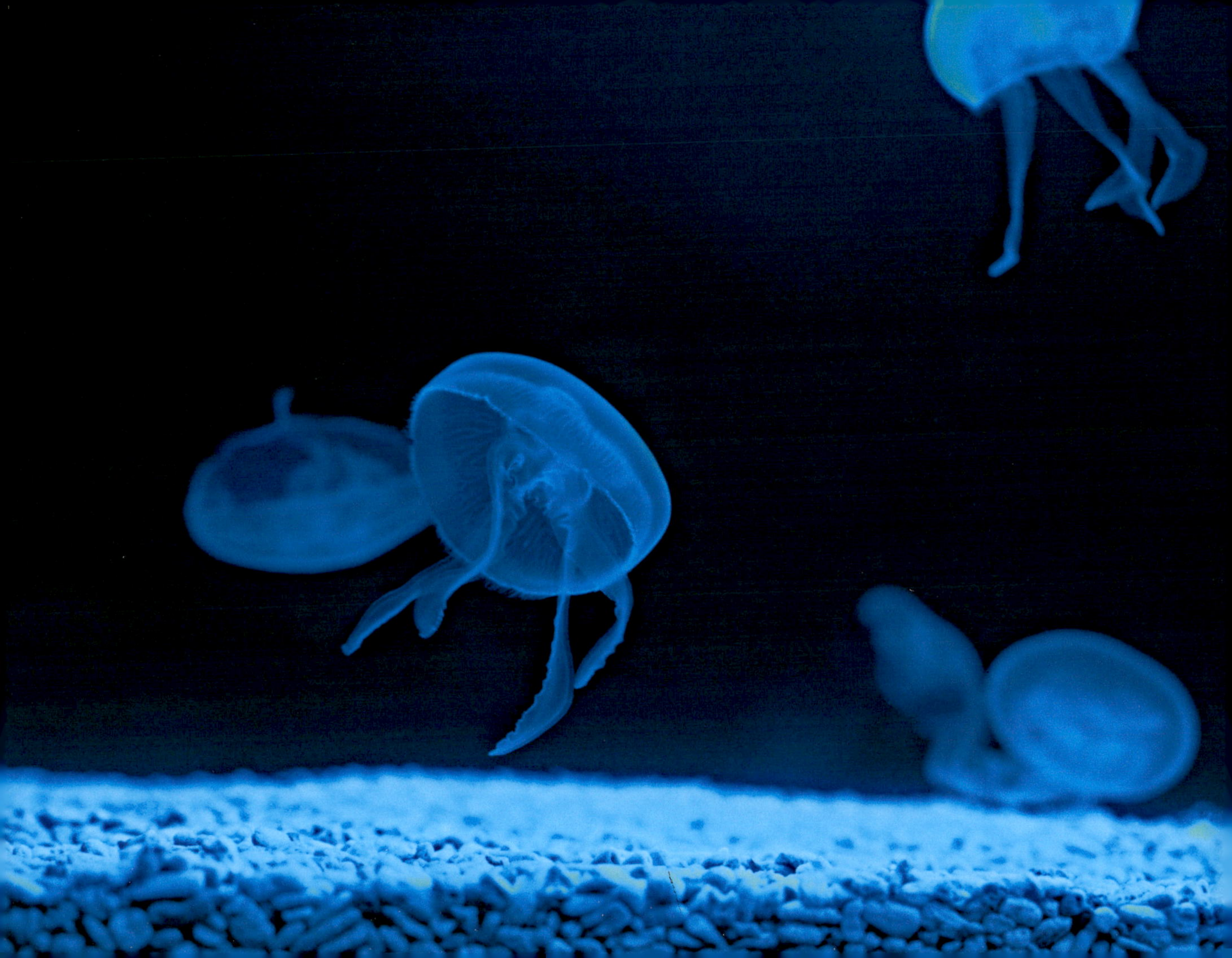

«angenommen, wir verbringen aus ökologischen gründen unser gesamtes leben mit denselben produkten?» – «stillstand ist keine lösung. wir wissen, daß wir aus ökonomischen gründen geschwindigkeit brauchen.» – «geht es denn wenigstens darum, den lebenszyklus der produkte zu verlängern?» – «das ist selbstverständlich. es ist wichtig für jedes unternehmen, daß sich seine investitionen für einen langen zeitraum bezahlt machen.» – «also aus jedem produkt einen designklassiker machen?» – «das läßt sich nicht planen. nur ein produkt, das den zeitgeist in seinen absichten, ressourcen und medien, mit seinem ausdruck, material und kulturellen erbe und in seiner technik am besten einfängt, kann zum klassiker werden.»

«Let's assume that, for ecological reasons, we spend our entire lives with the same products.» – «Standing still is not a solution. We know that we need speed for economic reasons.» – «Is the aim then at least to prolong the life cycle of products?» – «That is a matter of course. It's important for every business that its investments should pay for a long period.» – «So every product has to be made a design classic?» – «That can't be planned. Only a product that captures the spirit of the times in its intentions, resources and media, with its expression, material, cultural heritage and technology can become a classic.»

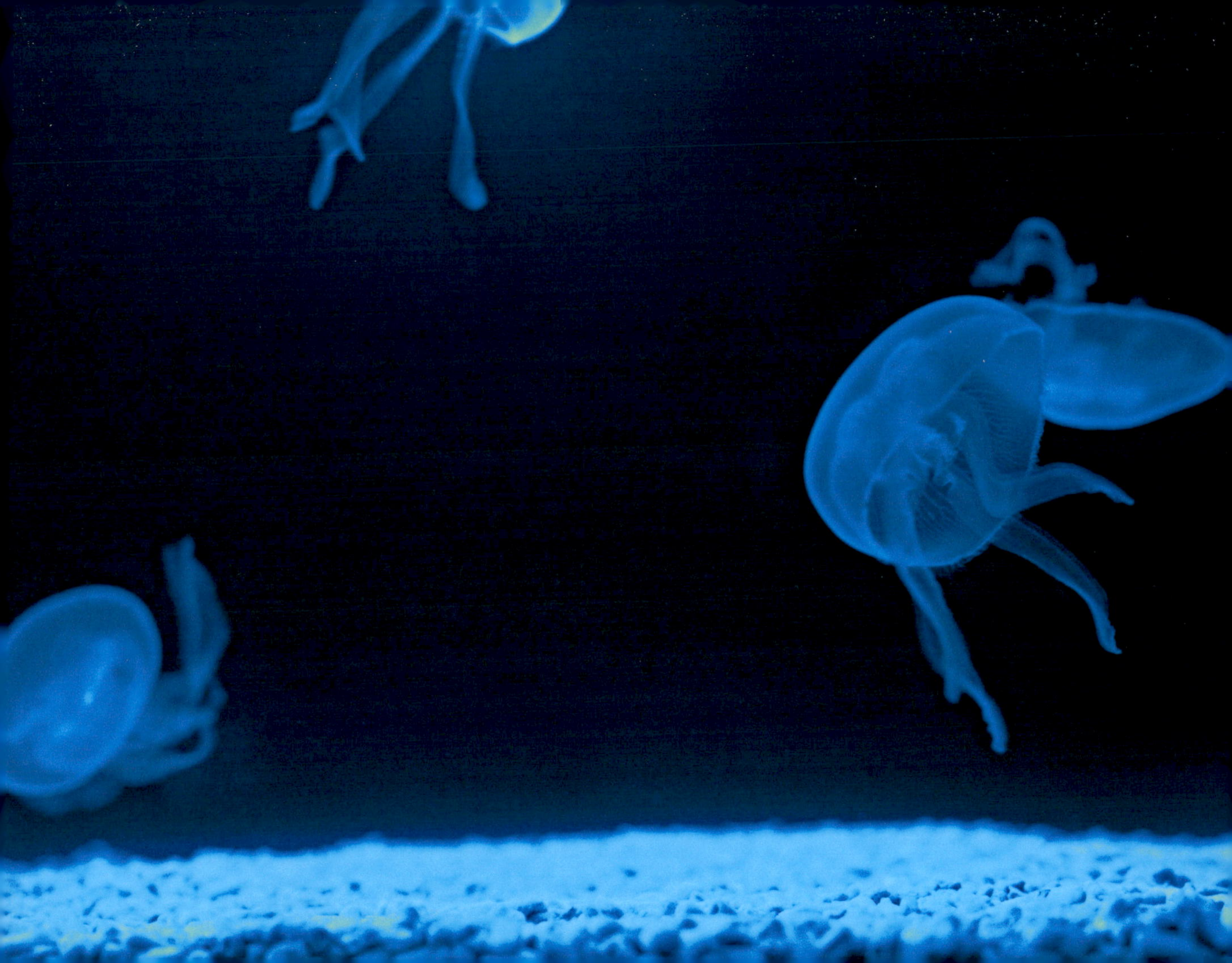

«die aufgabe des unternehmens, wenn es doch darum geht, sich dem designklassiker anzunähern?» – «aussortieren. grenzen durchbrechen. nicht reflexartig den kosmetischen trends folgen.»

«What do companies have to do to if the aim is to get as close as possible to a design classic?» – «Sort things out. Break through barriers. Not just follow the cosmetic trends as a reflex action.»

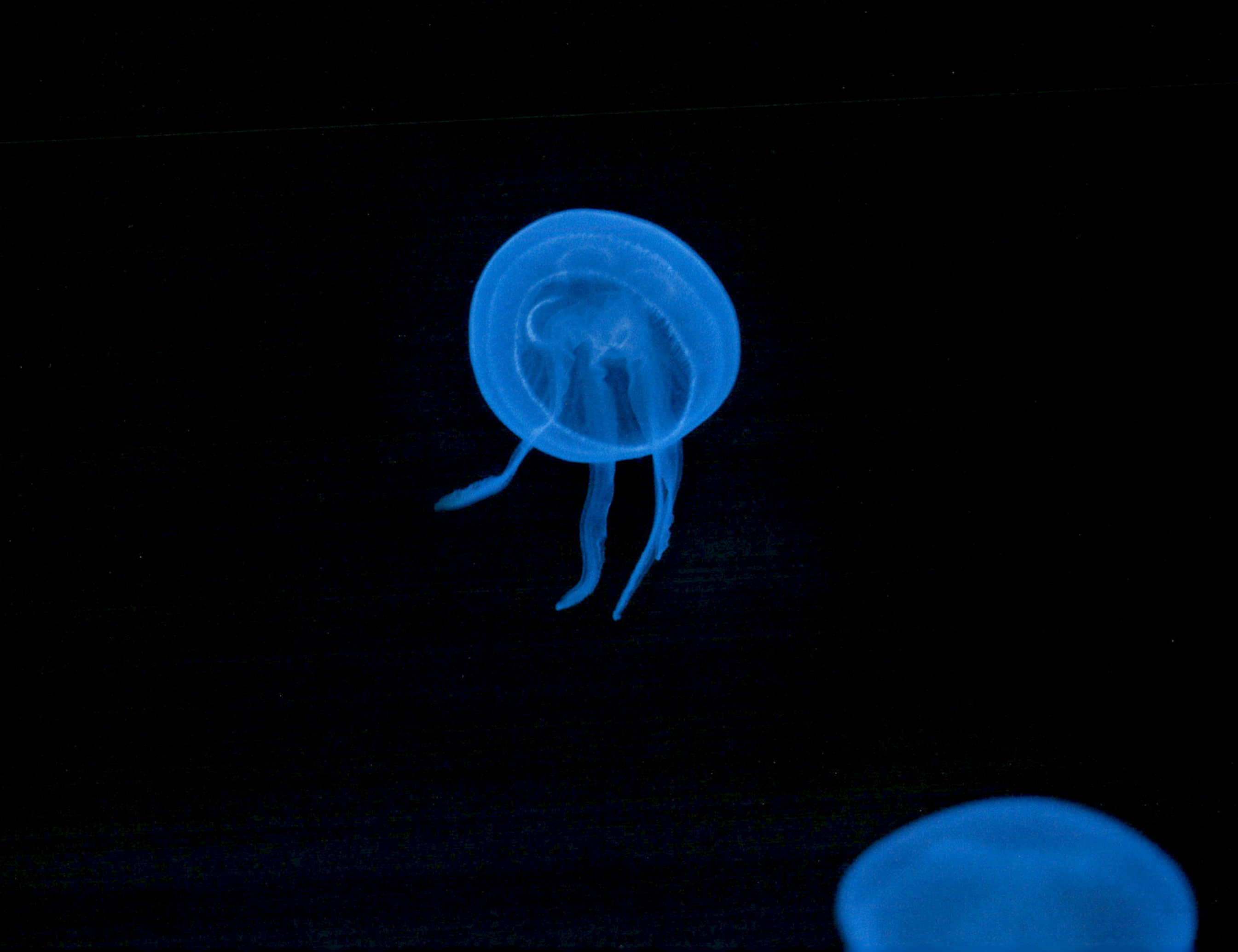

«zeitlosigkeit ist eine erstrebenswerte kategorie im design.» – «das konzept der zeitlosigkeit ist eine oberflächliche erfindung. wer sich gedanken über die heutige gesellschaft macht, hat erfolgschancen. mach deine hausaufgaben, dann wird dein produkt länger erfolg haben.» – «wie wird der designklassiker als ergebnis der bewegung durch die gelbe passage aussehen?» – «er wird unbeabsichtigt hervorgehen. ein designklassiker kann nicht mit der absicht entworfen werden, eben einen solchen zu schaffen.»

«Timelessness is a desirable category in design.» – «The concept of timelessness is a superficial invention. If you think about today's society you have a chance of success. Do your homework, and the product will be successful for longer.» – «What will the design classic that results from moving along the yellow passage look like?» – «It will emerge unintentionally. You can't design a classic by intending to design one.»

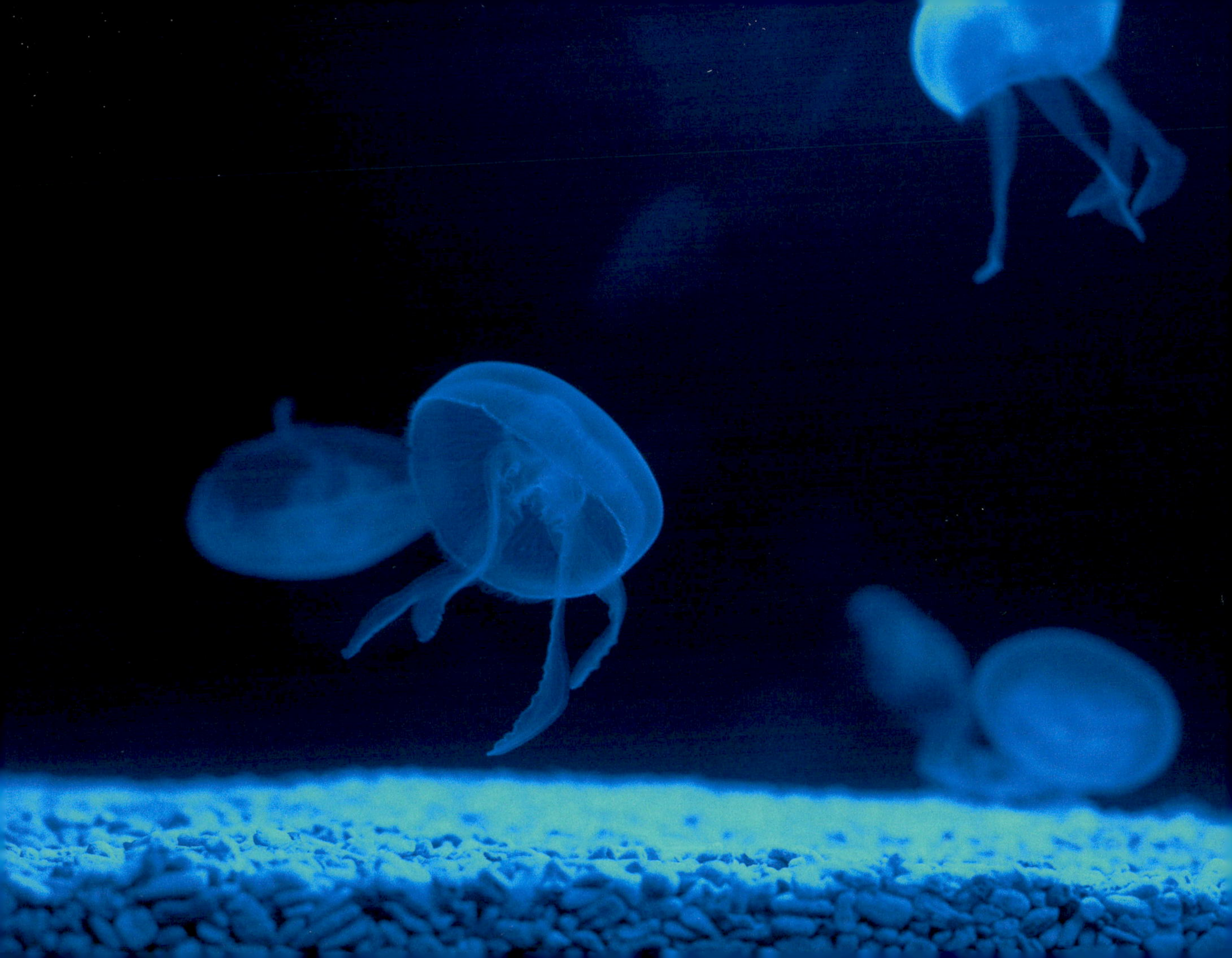

«die beziehung zwischen dem markt und einem unternehmen entspricht der beziehung zweier menschen. es gibt keinen unterschied. der begriff ‹marke› ist nur eine moderne beschreibung für einen sinnvollen und nachhaltigen dialog, der auf gegenseitigem verständnis und gleichen werten beruht.»

«The relationship between the market and a company is equivalent to the relationship between two people. There is no difference. The term ‹brand› is just a modern description of a sensible, sustained dialogue based on mutual understanding and common values.»

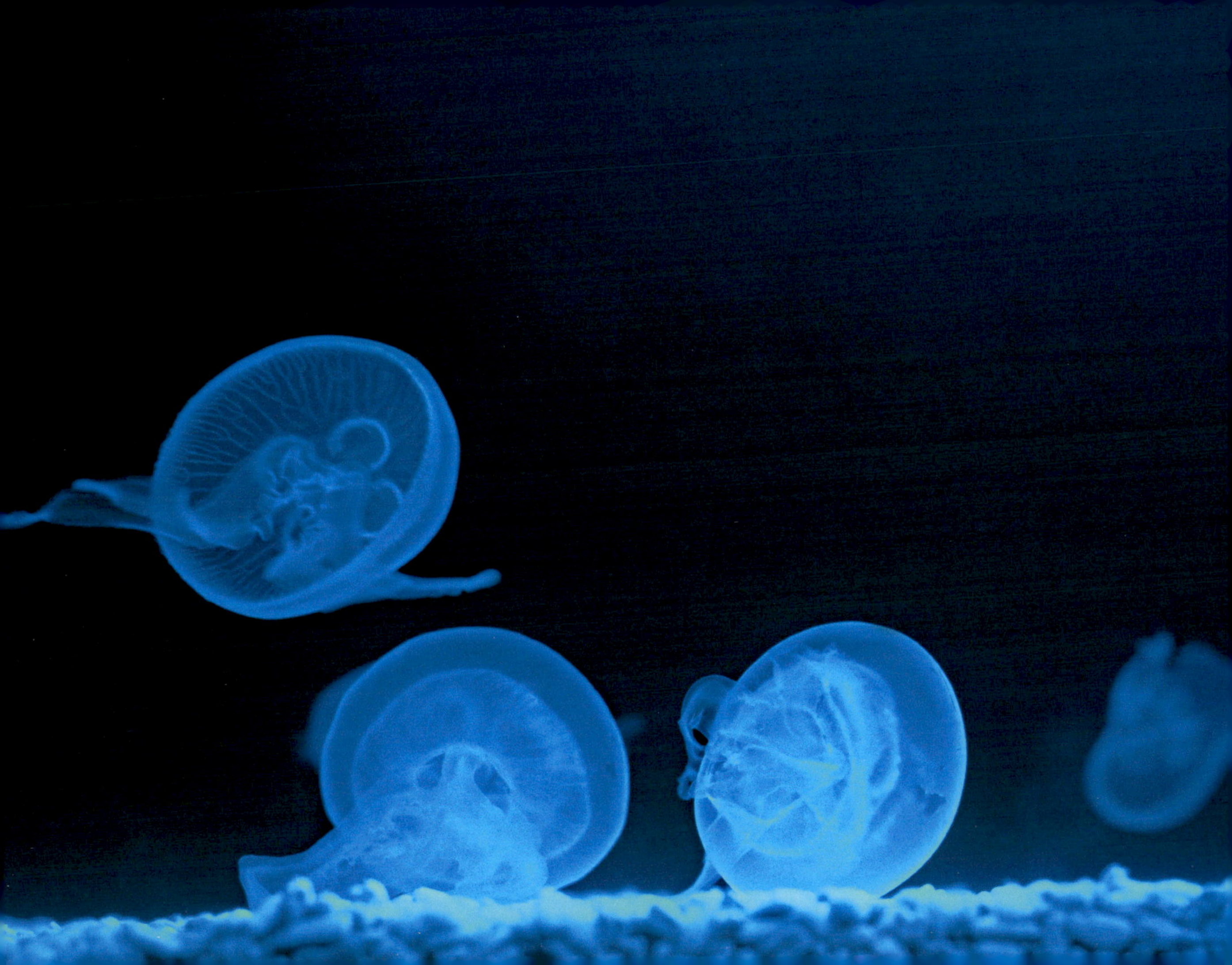

«braucht der designer die eingebung?» – «auch wer strategisch arbeitet, kann auf intuition nicht verzichten. intuition ist teil der strategie.»

«Do designers need intuition?» – «Even if you work strategically, you can't do without intuition. Intuition is part of the strategy.»

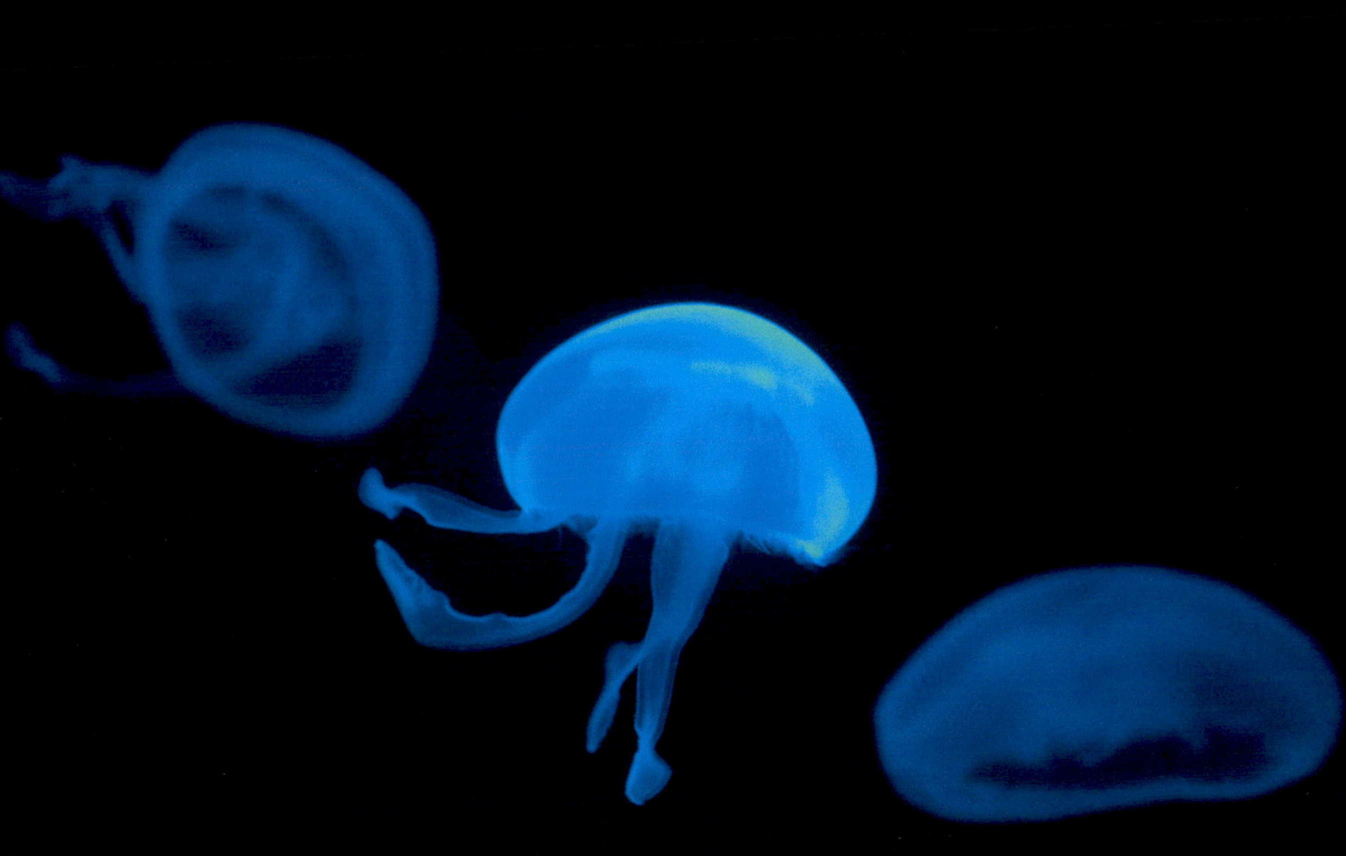

«wie groß war der intuitive anteil bei diesem entwurf?» – «die gesamte installation war eine eingebung. aber ich kann sie erklären. und solange ihre ergebnisse begründet werden können, ist intuition gut. wir müssen allerdings noch einmal zurückgehen und die idee hinterfragen. wenn man gelernt hat, zu erklären, warum ein bestimmtes design gewählt wurde, dann wird die diskussion erheblich fruchtbarer als wenn man nur stur behauptet, das design sei hübsch.» – «ist intuition also ein element, das designer und unternehmen verbindet?» – «designer und unternehmen sprechen nicht dieselbe sprache. die strategie bildet deswegen eine gemeinsame grundlage zur verständigung, um eine idee zu kommunizieren.» – «die strategie als design-interpret?»

«How big a part did intuition play in this design?» – «The entire installation was intuition, but I can explain it, and as long as the results can be justified, intuition is a good thing. Nevertheless, we have to go back and question the idea. When you have learned how to explain why a particular design was selected, the discussion is considerably more productive than if you just stubbornly assert that the design is pretty.» – «So is intuition something that links designers and companies?» – «Designers and companies don't speak the same language. That's why the strategy creates a common ground for understanding and for communication of an idea.» – «Strategy as an interpreter of design?»

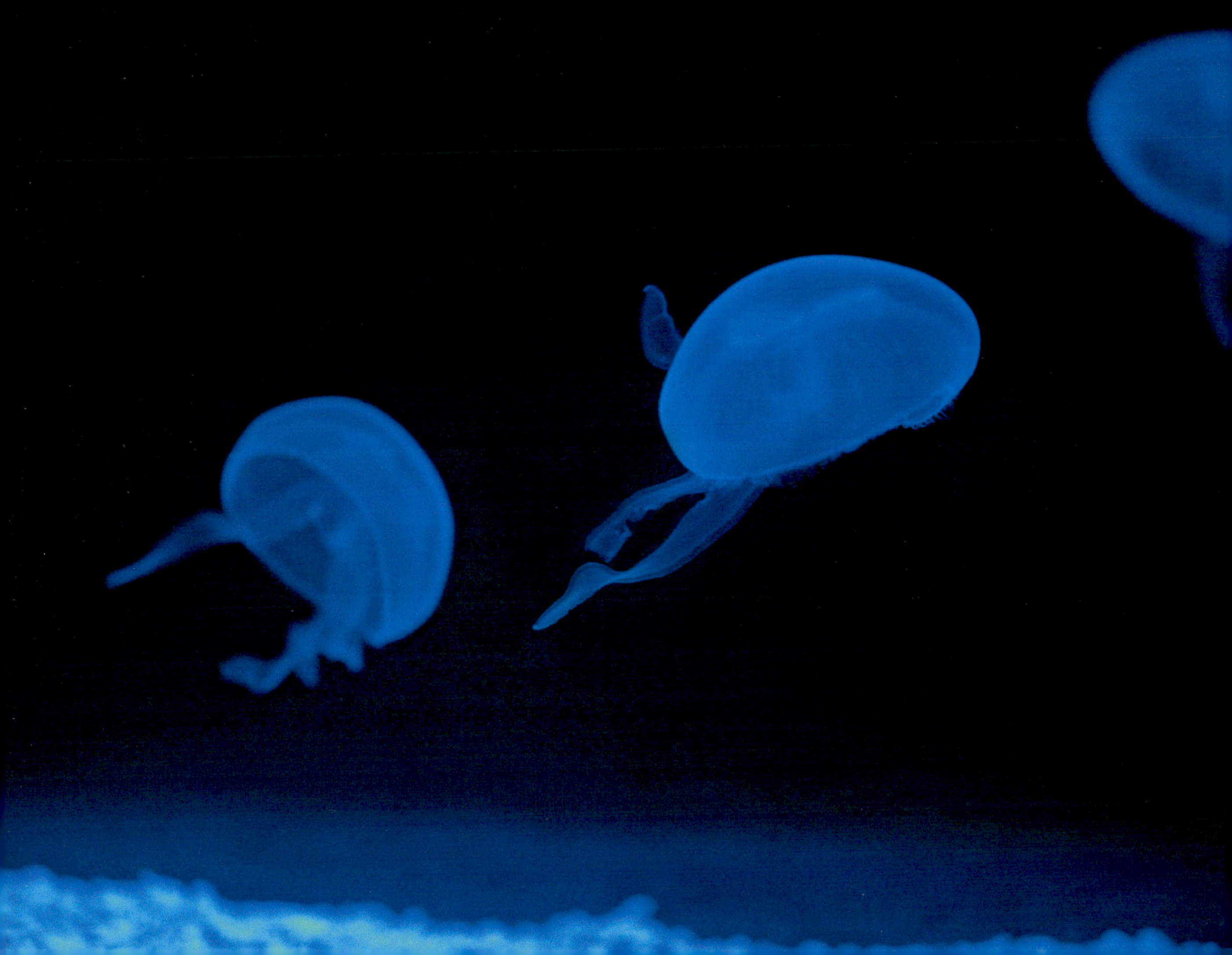

«erfahrungsreichtum stimuliert eingebungen?» – «darum ist es so wichtig, ein möglichst breites spektrum an erfahrungen und wissen zu sammeln. sie alle dienen als quelle der intuition. wer sich nur auf den ausgetretenen weg des wissens begibt, auf dem sich alle bewegen, wird auch nur altbekannte zahlen und daten hervorbringen.»

«Does a richness of experience stimulate intuition?» – «That's why it's so important to gain as broad a spectrum of knowledge and experience as possible. All that is a source of intuition. If you just keep to the beaten track of what everybody knows, you will only be able to produce the old familiar facts and figures.»

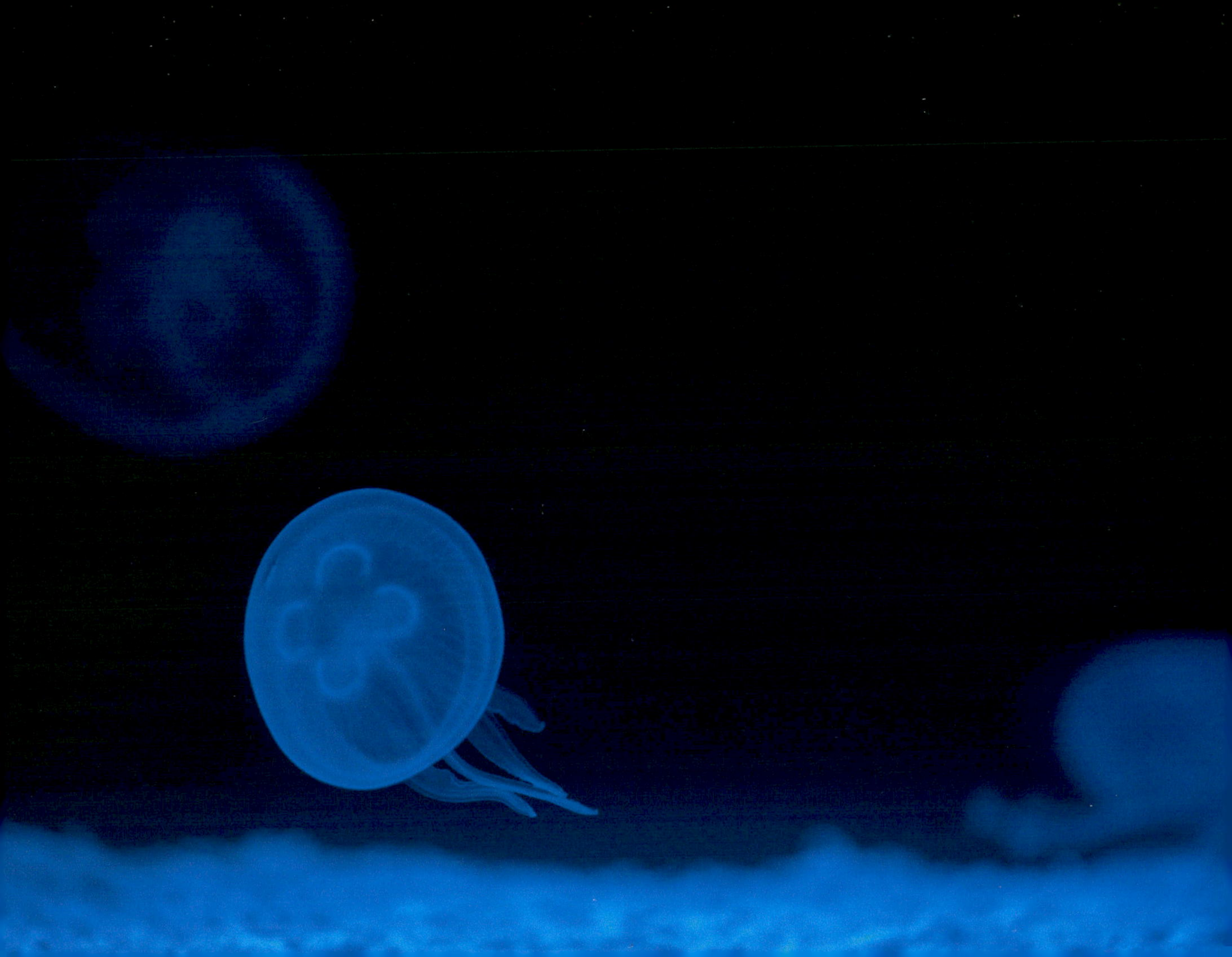

«intuition gibt es auch in der geschäftswelt.» – «es geht stets darum, daß intuition auf erfahrung beruht. dadurch wird intuition noch kein planungsinstrument, aber sie ist rationaler als es den anschein hat. wer erfolgreich sein und sein publikum überraschen will, muß intuition fördern. die wirklichen chancen sind nicht durch zahlen und daten abgesichert.»

«There's intuition in the business world too.» – «Intuition is always based on experience. That doesn't make intuition a planning tool, but it is more rational than it seems. People who want to be successful and surprise their audiences have to promote intuition. The real opportunities don't come from facts and figures alone.»

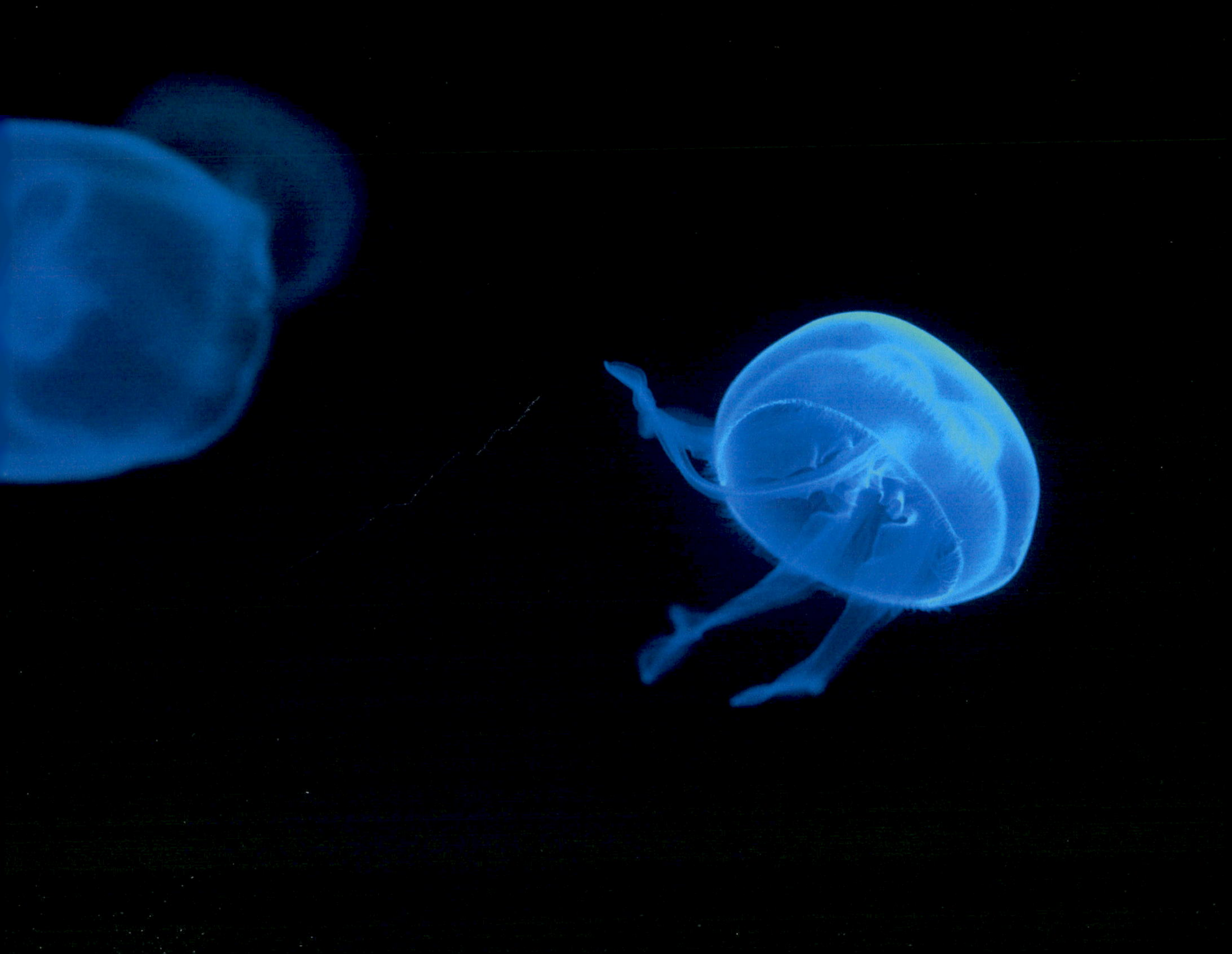

«läßt sich der designprozeß, läßt sich intuition mit einem ‹briefing› in auftrag geben?» – «zum einen wird der designprozeß mystifiziert. zum anderen sind die meisten unternehmen nicht dazu in der lage, einen auftrag angemessen zu formulieren.»

«Can the design process, can intuition be ordered in a briefing?» – «On the one hand, the design process is mystified there. On the other hand, most companies are not capable of formulating a design brief properly.»

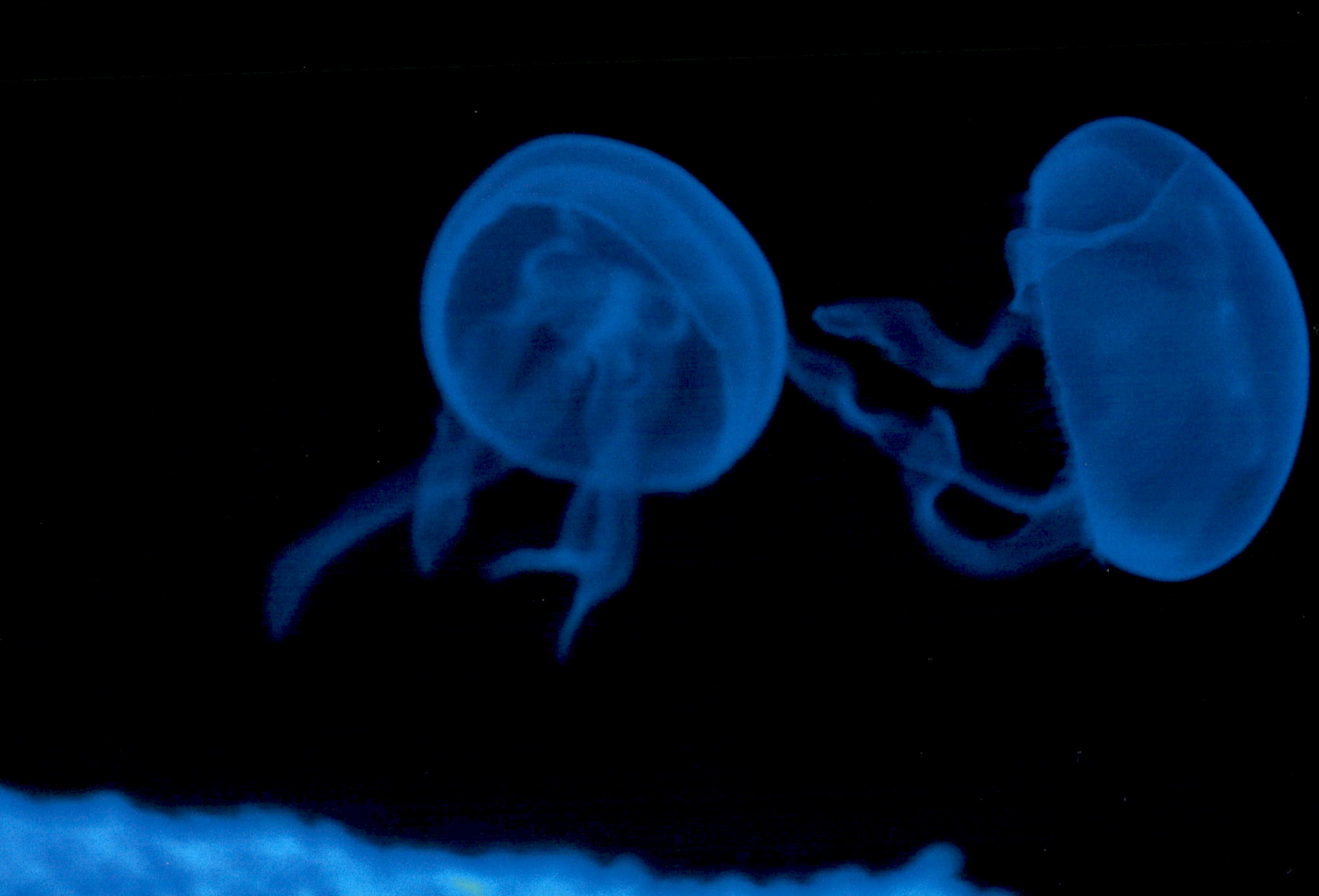

«ist der designer als gesprächspartner seines auftraggebers, welcher ein kaufmann ist, noch glaubwürdig, wenn er mit intuition argumentiert?» – «es muß ihm gelingen, den grund für seine intuition darzustellen. dann erhält er die rationale bestätigung für seine eingebung.»

«Is the designer still a credible partner in discussions with his client when he argues in terms of intuition?» – «He has to manage to explain the reasons for his intuition, and then his inspiration is rationally confirmed.»

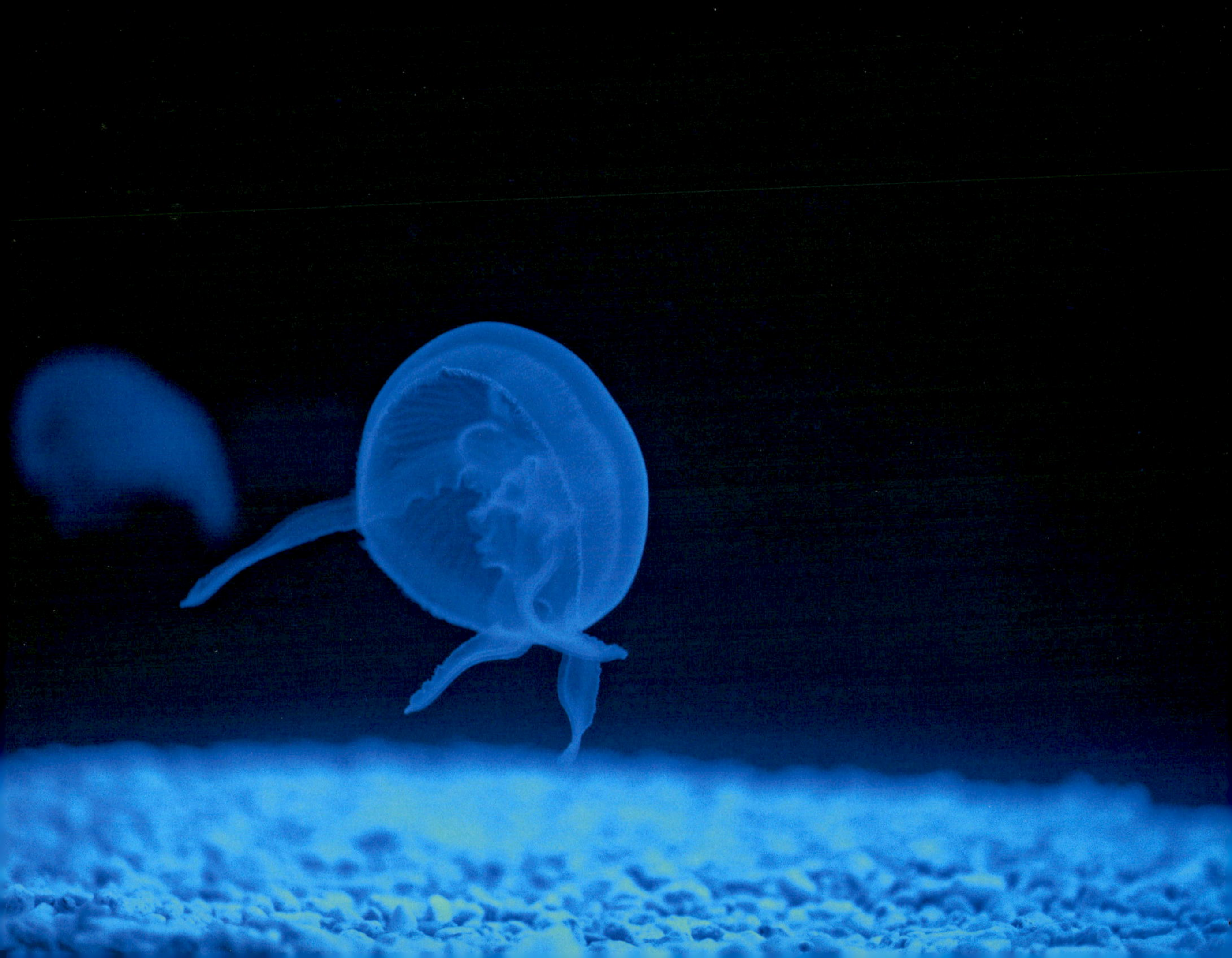

«wo zeigt sich die schönheit: im entwurfsprozeß oder im ergebnis?» – «wo zeigt sich das ergebnis des entwurfsprozesses: innen oder außen?»

«Where is the beauty: in the process or in the result?» – «Where is the result of the design process: on the inside or the outside?»

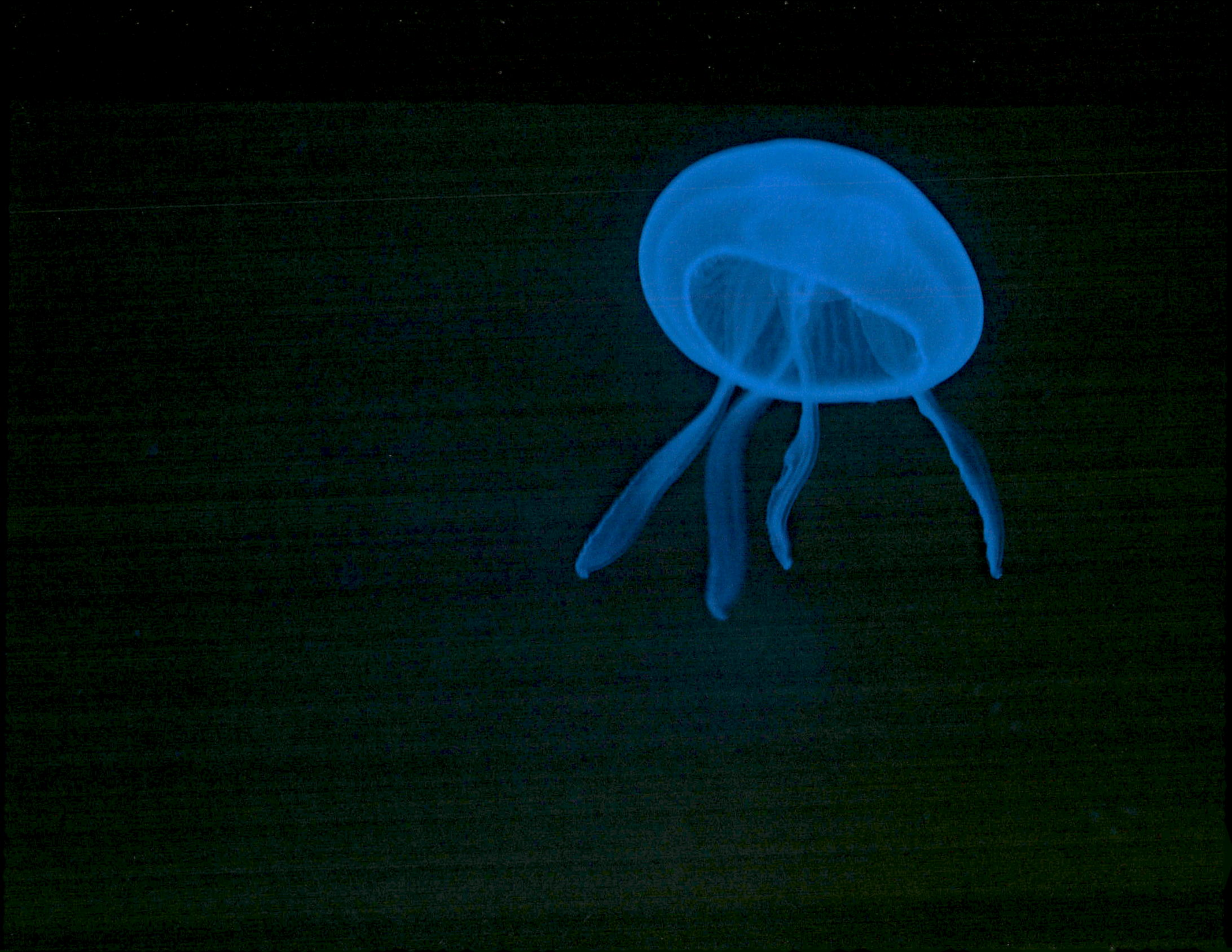

«ich glaube nicht, daß wir uns jemals dem auch nur annähern, was die natur vermag, wenn es um meine persönliche vorstellung von perfekter ästhetik geht.»

«I don't believe that we'll ever be able to come close to what happens biologically in nature when it comes to my subjective idea of what is perfect aesthetics.»

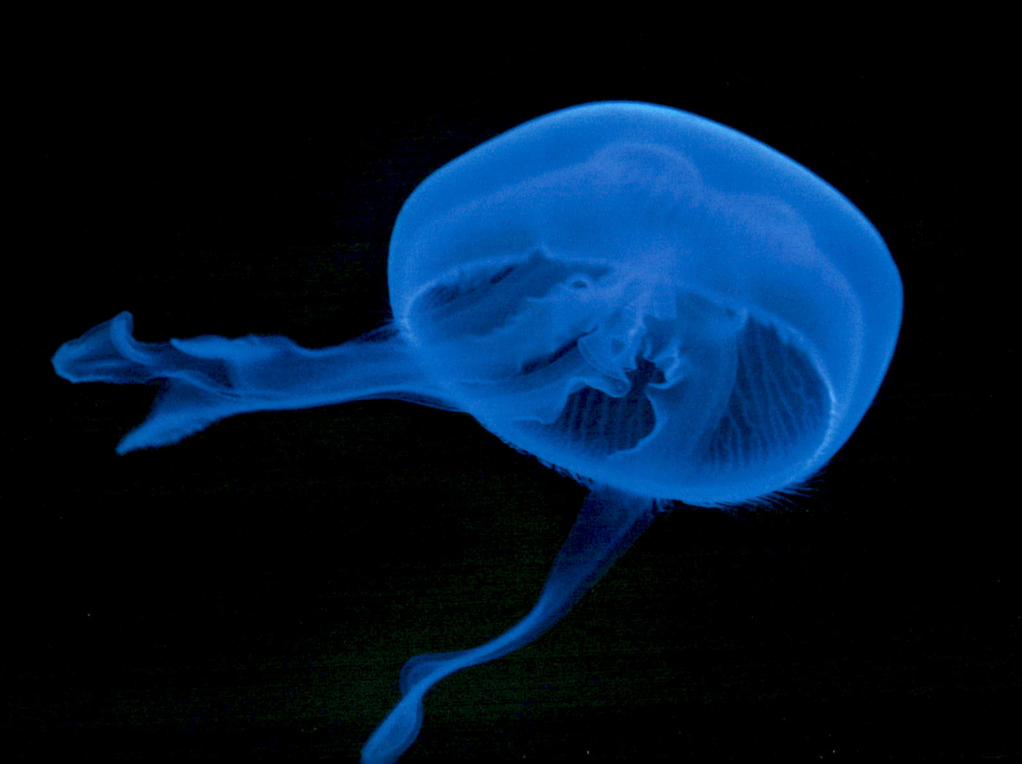

es ist egal, wie schön du bist. dein leben kann trotzdem langweilig sein.

It doesn't matter how beautiful you are. Life can still be boring.

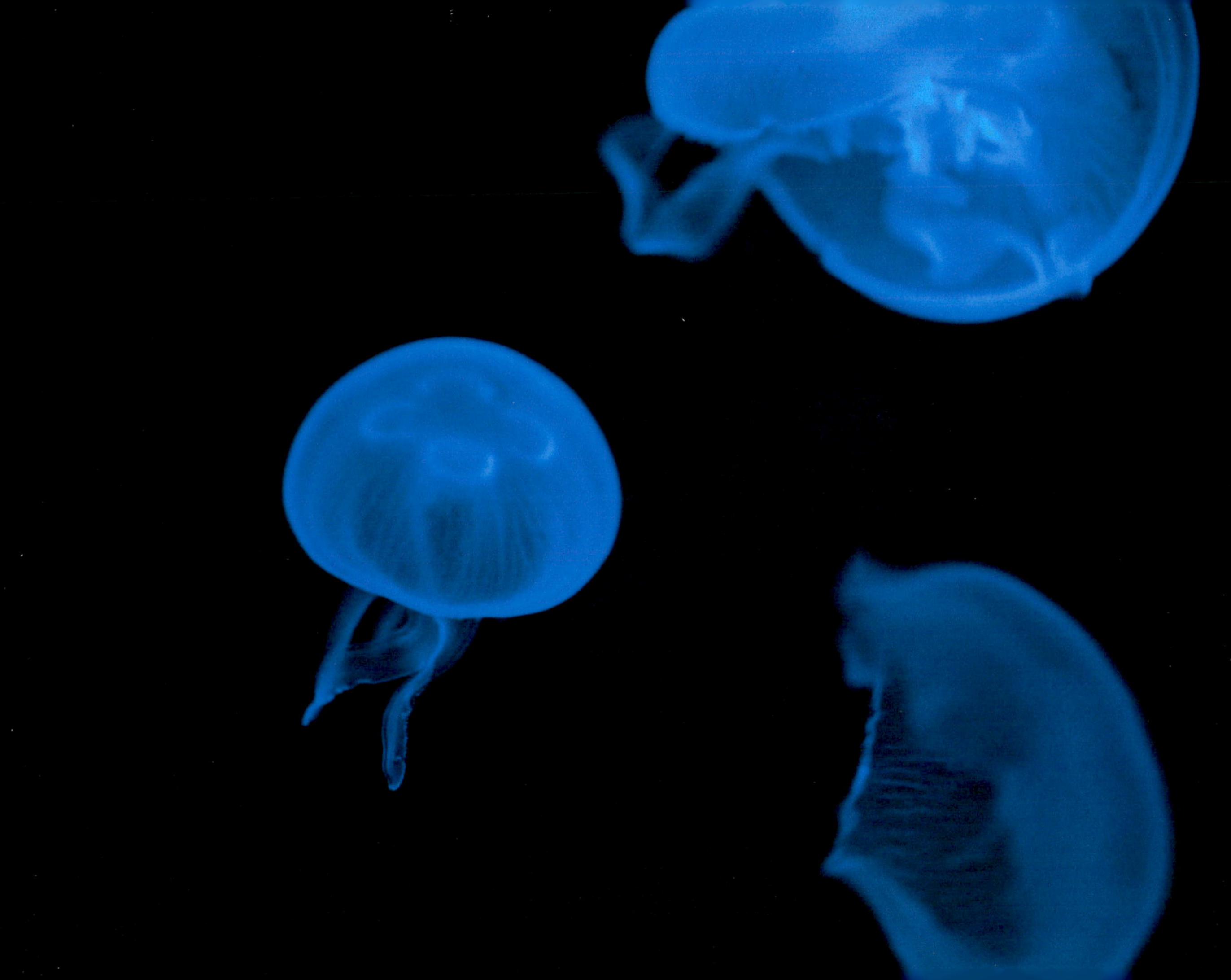

«plasticbag theme» von thomas newman,
aus dem film «american beauty»

das lied wurde zum tanzen geschrieben, ganz gleich, ob man eine qualle oder eine plastiktüte ist.

«Plasticbag theme» by Thomas Newman
from the movie «American beauty»

It's a song made for dancing, whether you're a jellyfish or a plastic bag.

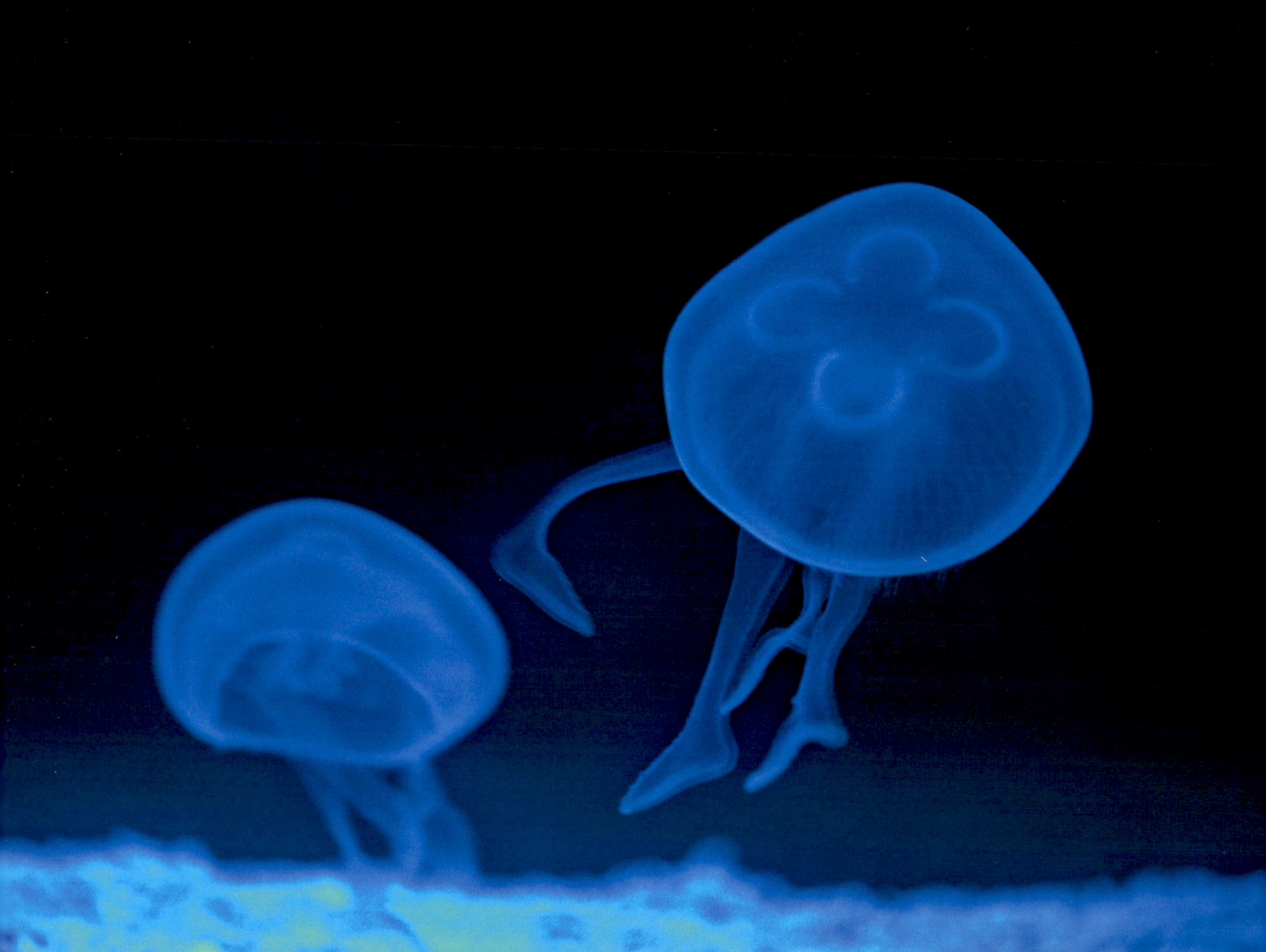

kurz vor drucklegung dieses buches entdeckt der experte eine aquaristische sensation: unzählbar viele polypen im aquarium. jeder nur stecknadelkopfgroß. das wasser voller organismen. zudem ein paar handvoll (im numerischen, nicht im wörtlichen sinn) ebenso kleine quallen als jungfernzeugungen, also exakte reproduktionen der lebewesen, von denen sie stammen. natürliches klonen. die elterlichen quallen hatten sich vorerst doch nur an einem tag im installationsaquarium aufgehalten. an einem tag im frühen november, als diese fotos aufgenommen wurden. kaum gelegenheit, sich häuslich einzurichten.

«läßt sich identifizieren, von welcher qualle die polypen abstammen?» – «nein.» – «ist es ein zeichen von streß, von existentieller bedrohung, daß sich die quallen so rasch um die erhaltung ihrer art gekümmert haben?» – «es gibt wohl drei verschiedene reize, die die quallen dazu veranlassen, tausende eier zu legen. vermutlich waren es hier optimale äußere verhältnisse, erzeugt für die mediengesellschaftliche notwendigkeit, so früh wie möglich fotos für dieses buch und für die pressemitteilungen aufnehmen zu können.» – «fotografieren fördert den fortbestand der sippe?»

Shortly before this book went to print, our expert advisor discovered an aquatic sensation: countless polyps in the aquarium, all of them no larger than a pinhead, and the water full of organisms. There were also a few handfuls (in the numerical sense, not literally) of just as small medusae as asexual, exact reproductions of the beings they stemmed from. Natural cloning. The parent jellyfish had previously only spent a single day in the installation aquarium – a day in early November, when these photos were taken. Hardly time to set up a household.

«Can we tell which jellyfish the polyps come from?» – «No.» – «Is it a sign of stress, of some existential threat, that the jellyfish have worked on the survival of their species so quickly?» – «There are three different stimuli which cause the jellyfish to lay thousands of eggs. In this case, presumably, it was the optimum external conditions brought about by the need of the media society to produce photos for this book and the press releases as soon as possible.» – «Does being photographed promote the survival of the race?»

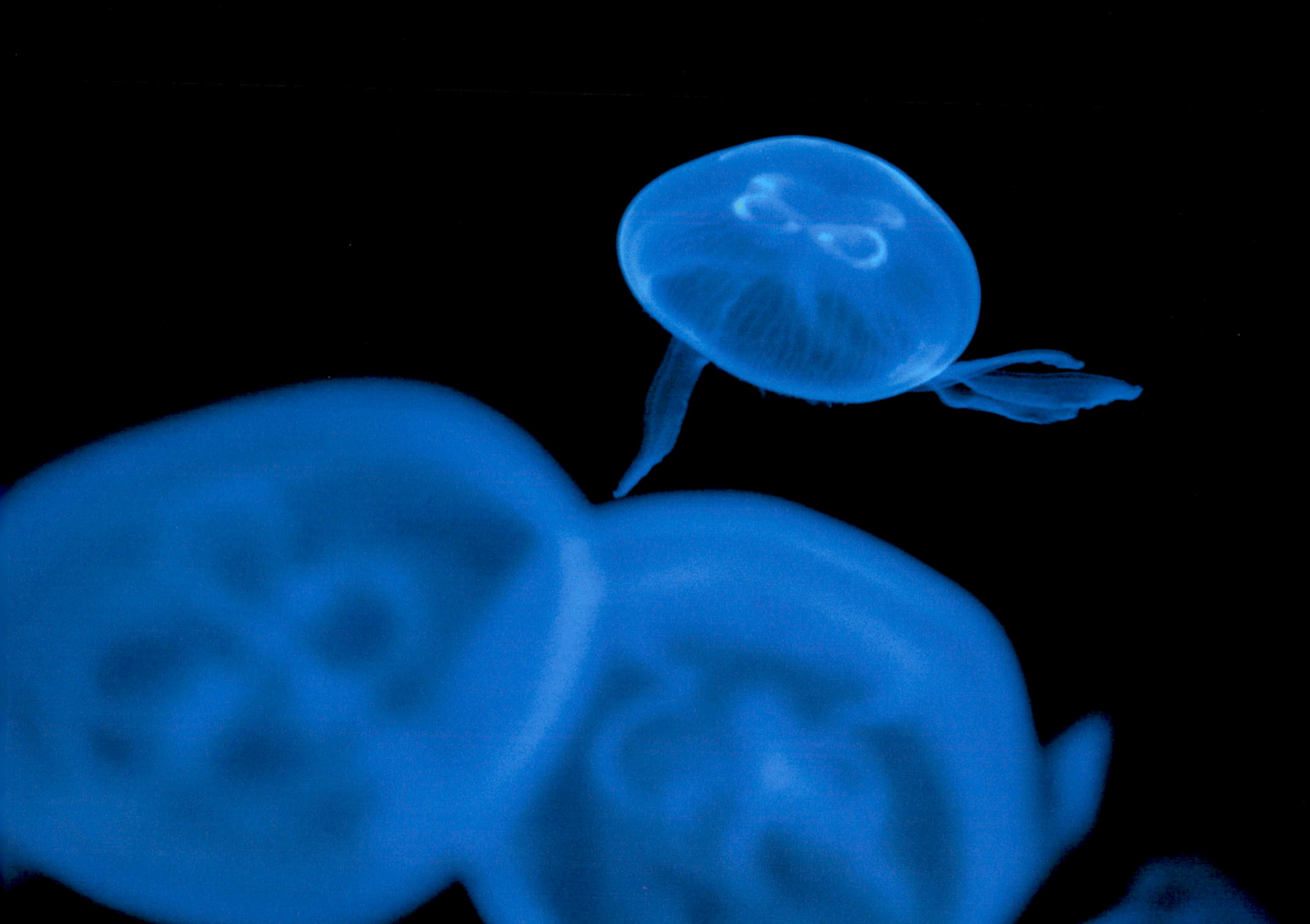

noch im spätsommer war es mehrere wochen lang als aussichtslos erschienen, auch nur ein dutzend quallen für die ausstellung auszuleihen. die technischen voraussetzungen zu erfüllen, die für das artenkonforme leben der tiere notwendig sind, erschien ebenso unmöglich. als es gegen alle prognosen zustande gebracht war, etablierte sich augenblicklich eine originäre eigelstein-zucht. – räsonnieren darüber, was mit den entwürfen geschieht, die man durch ihre verwirklichung in die welt setzt. fruchtbarkeit von ideen an ecken und enden, von denen man es nicht erwartet hätte. eigendynamik, unkontrollierbar. vermessenheit des designers, die gestaltung der welt in allen dimensionen, in der tragweite ihrer physischen existenz, kontrollieren zu können.

Even in late summer, there had for several weeks appeared to be no prospects of borrowing even a dozen jellyfish. Fulfilling the technical conditions required to keep them in a suitable environment seemed just as impossible. When, against all expectations, it had been done, an original Eigelstein breed established itself immediately. Grounds to philosophise about what happens to designs which emerge into the world. Fertility of ideas in nooks and crannies where it had least been expected. A self-driven, uncontrollable dynamism. The presumption of designers to think they could control the design of the world in all its dimensions, in all the purport of its physical existence.

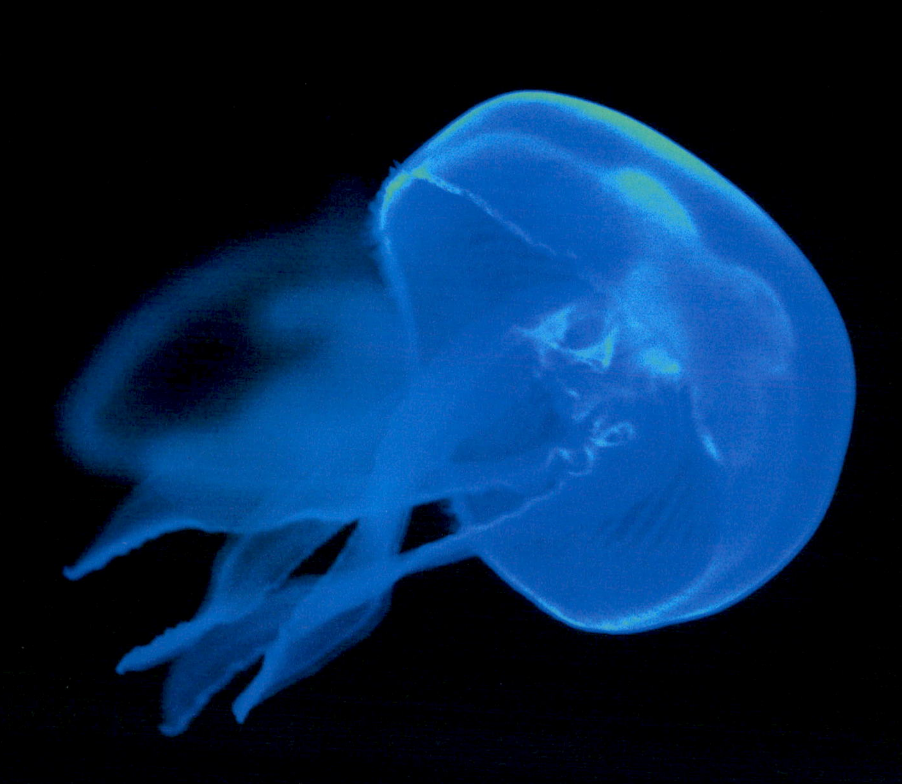

zeit. raum. schwerkraft.

Time. Space. Gravity.

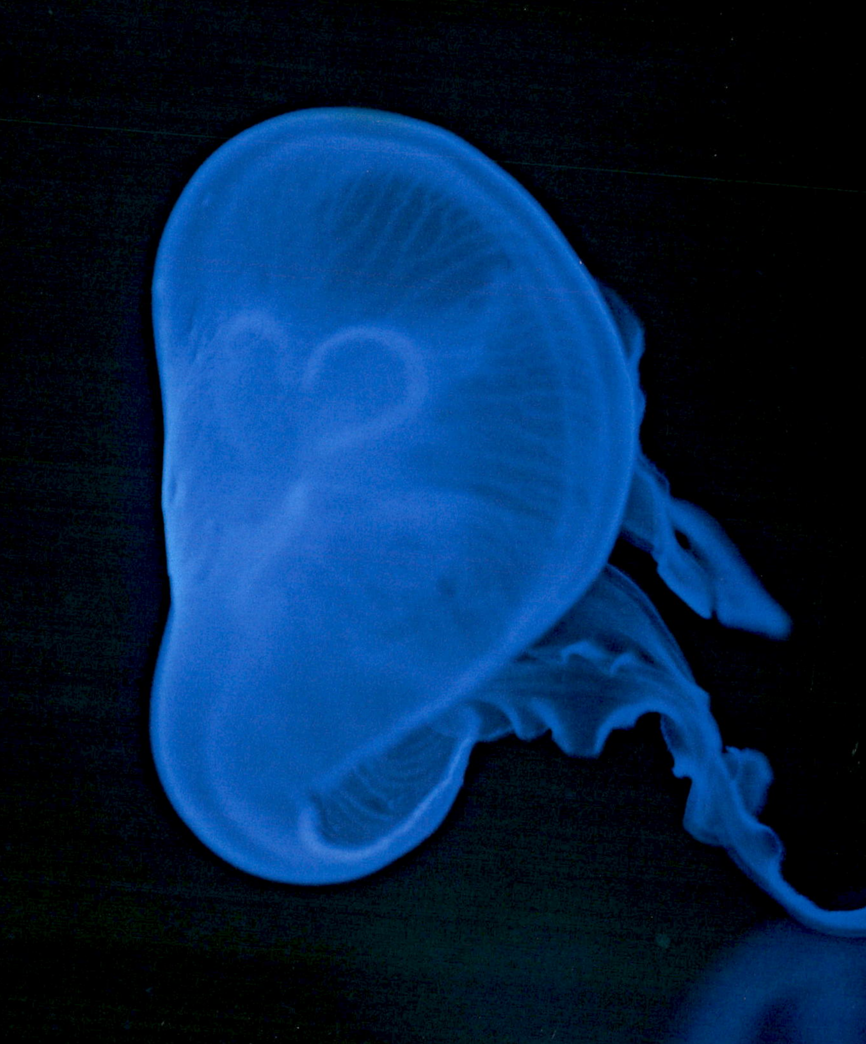

alberto alessi ron arad antonia astori françois azambourg enrico baleri johnson banks fabien baron françois bauchet baumann & baumann ruedi baur martine bedin mario bellini sebastien bergne jeffrey bernett marc berthier christian biecher ayse birsel philippe boisselier ronan & erwan bouroullec constantin boym andreas brandolini andrea branzi julian brown tim brown christoph burckardt & albrecht hotz philippe chaix & jean-paul morel antonio citterio mårten claesson eero koivisto ola rune sheridan coackley denis colomb terence conran matali crasset chris deam philippe delis the designers republic design hoch drei tom dixon marie-christine dorner droog design sylvain dubuisson rena dumas studio dumbar james dyson li edelkoort factor design farrow design thomas feicht patricia fletcher oscar fuentes naoto fukasawa elisabeth garouste & mattia bonetti kristian gavoile gérard gayoud stephano giovannoni johanna grawunder konstantin grcic marti guixé alfredo häberli sam hecht hesse designstudios fons m. hickmann matthew hilton takenobu igarashi imagination in/corporate interbrand zintzmeier & lux james irvine hella jongerius eric jourdan patrick jouin perry king & santagio miranda kms team claus koch masayuki kurokawa jean-philippe lenclos leptien 3 uwe loesch pippo lioni piero lissoni ross lovegrove michele de lucchi vico magistretti thomas manss christophe marchand enzo mari javier mariscal jean-marie massaud mastrangello tatsuya matsui jean-claude maugirard john maeda ingo maurer alberto meda marc meiré allessandro mendini jasper morrisson murray moss pascal mourgue ted muehling michael nash navyblue nemo, alain domingo & françois scali marc newson nordisk ora ito lippa pearce richard peduzzi pentagram jorge pensi atelier roger pfund christoph pillet seymour & powell andrée putman dieter rams karim rashid paolo rizzatto patrick & daniel rubin marc sadler timo salli eduardo samso sandellsandberg denis santachiara richard sapper afra bianchin & tobia scarpa peter schmidt scholz & volkmer maarten van severen dieter sieger borek sipek snowcrash ettore sottsass erik spiekermann philippe starck peter stathis stockholm design lab martin szekely roger tallon matteo thun oscar tusquets paolo ulian shigeru uchida oliver vogt & hermann weizenegger kurt weidemann hannes wettstein jean-michel wilmotte syunji yamanaka sori yanagi tokujin yoshioka michael young stefan ytterborn marco zanuso